201
COOKIES

201 COOKIES

Tasty, Tempting, Toothsome Treats

201 Delicious Recipes
201 Tantalizing Pictures

BY GREGG R. GILLESPIE

BLACK DOG
& LEVENTHAL
PUBLISHERS
NEW YORK

Published by
Black Dog & Leventhal Publishers, Inc.
151 West 19th Street
New York, NY 10011

Distributed by
Workman Publishing Company
708 Broadway
New York, NY 10003

Manufactured in The United Kingdom

Gillespie, Gregg R., 1934–
201 cookies / by Gregg R. Gillespie.
p. cm.

ISBN: 1-57912-115-2
1. Cookies I. Title
TX771 .G43 2000
641.8'654--dc21

j i h g f e d c

TABLE OF CONTENTS

COOKIES A–Z 1

INGREDIENTS

    NUTS 104

    FRUITS 105

    SPICES AND HERBS 106

    CHOCOLATE 108

    MISCELLANEOUS 109

    FLAVORINGS 110

ALTERNATIVE FLAVORINGS 111

PANTRY

    FROSTINGS AND ICINGS.................113

    FILLINGS 115

    BAR COOKIE CRUSTS....................116

COOKIES
A-Z

ABERNATHY BISCUITS

Rolled Cookies

YIELD: *2 to 3 dozen*
TOTAL TIME: *30 minutes*

5½ cups all-purpose flour
1½ cups granulated sugar
1½ teaspoons baking powder
1½ cups vegetable shortening
3 large eggs
3 tablespoons milk, or more if needed
3 tablespoons caraway seeds
1½ teaspoons grated lemon zest

1 Preheat the oven to 375 degrees.

2 In a large bowl, combine the flour, sugar, and baking powder. Cut in the shortening until the mixture resembles coarse crumbs.

3 In another bowl, beat the eggs, milk, caraway seeds, and lemon zest until well blended. Blend into the dry ingredients until smooth. If the dough seems too stiff, add a little more milk 1 teaspoon at a time.

4 On a floured surface, roll out the dough ¼ inch thick. Using a 2-inch round cookie cutter, cut out cookies and place 1½ inches apart on ungreased baking sheets.

5 Bake for 7 to 10 minutes, until the edges are lightly browned. Transfer to wire racks to cool.

Baking notes: Sweet creams or a lemon sugar frosting can be drizzled over the tops of these cookies, or they can be served plain at teatime with jam or preserves. For variation, this dough can be rolled out to a thickness of ⅛ inch and used to make sandwich cookies. The filling can be melted chocolate or a thick lemon custard. (See Pantry for recipes.)

AFGHANS

Formed Cookies

YIELD: *3 to 4 dozen*
TOTAL TIME: *30 minutes*

⅓ cup pitted dates, chopped fine
½ cup boiling water, or more to cover dates
1 cup all-purpose flour
¼ cup unsweetened cocoa powder
1 teaspoon baking powder
¾ cup vegetable shortening
¼ cup granulated sugar
1 teaspoon vanilla extract
2 cups cornflakes

1 Preheat the oven to 350 degrees.

2 Place the chopped dates in a small cup and cover with the boiling water for 10 to 15 minutes. Drain and discard the liquid.

3 Combine the flour, cocoa, and baking powder.

4 In a large bowl, cream the vegetable shortening and sugar until light and fluffy. Stir in the dates. Beat in the vanilla extract. Gradually blend in the dry ingredients. Fold in the cornflakes.

5 Break off walnut-sized pieces of the dough and roll into balls. Place 1½ inches apart on ungreased baking sheets.

6 Bake for 12 to 15 minutes, or until firm to the touch. Transfer to wire racks to cool.

Baking notes: The balls can be rolled in finely chopped nuts before baking. They can also be dredged in powdered sugar after baking, but these are quite sweet, so taste one before you decide to roll them in sugar.

ALMOND AWARDS

Bar Cookies
YIELD: *1 to 2 dozen*
TOTAL TIME: *50 minutes*

ALMOND BUTTER COOKIES

Formed Cookies
YIELD: *4 to 6 dozen*
TOTAL TIME: *35 minutes*

CRUST
1 cup all-purpose flour
½ teaspoon salt
½ cup vegetable shortening
½ cup granulated sugar
1 tablespoon grated lemon zest

TOPPING
½ cup vegetable shortening
½ cup granulated sugar
1 cup heavy cream
1 cup almonds, ground

1 Preheat the oven to 375 degrees. Lightly grease an 11 by 7-inch baking pan.
2 To make the crust, combine the flour and salt.
lemon zest. Gradually blend in the dry ingredients.
4 Press the dough evenly over the bottom of the prepared baking pan. Bake for 12 minutes. Transfer pan to wire rack to cool slightly.
5 Meanwhile, make the topping: Melt the shortening in a small saucepan. Stir in the sugar, cream, and almonds.
6 Spread the almond topping over the warm crust. Bake for 20 minutes longer, or until firm to the touch.
7 Cool in the pan on a wire rack before cutting into large or small bars.

2 cups all-purpose flour
1 teaspoon baking powder
1 cup butter, at room temperature
1 cup granulated sugar
2 large egg yolks
½ teaspoon lemon extract
¾ teaspoon almond extract
½ teaspoon vanilla extract
About 70 whole blanched almonds

1 Preheat the oven to 300 degrees.
2 Combine the flour and baking powder.
3 In a large bowl, cream the butter and sugar until light and fluffy. Beat in the egg yolks and the extracts. Blend in the dry ingredients.
4 Break off walnut-sized pieces of dough and roll into balls. Place 1½ inches apart on ungreased baking sheets.
5 Press an almond into the center of each cookie flattening them slightly. Bake for 15 to 20 minutes, until the cookies are golden brown. Transfer to wire racks to cool.

Almond Cakes

Formed Cookies

Yield: *5 to 6 dozen*
Total time: *30 minutes*

2 large eggs
1 cup granulated sugar
½ teaspoon vanilla extract
1 cup almonds, ground
1 cup all-purpose flour

1 Preheat the oven to 400 degrees. Lightly grease 2 baking sheets.

2 In a large bowl, beat the eggs until thick and light-colored. Beat in the sugar and vanilla extract. Beat in the almonds. Gradually blend in the flour.

3 Break off 1-inch pieces of dough and roll into balls. Place 2 inches apart on the prepared baking sheets.

4 Bake for 8 to 10 minutes, or until a light golden color. Transfer to wire racks to cool.

Baking notes: The balls of dough can be flattened and a half a glacé cherry or a nut pressed into each one before baking. Or, the cookies can be dipped in melted chocolate after they have cooled.

Almond Crescents

Formed Cookies

Yield: *2 to 4 dozen*
Total time: *30 minutes*

1 cup vegetable shortening
1 cup granulated sugar
1 large egg, separated
1 large egg yolk
4 hard-boiled large egg yolks, crumbled
1 tablespoon grated lemon zest
3 cups all-purpose flour
¼ cup almonds, ground
Granulated sugar for sprinkling

1 Preheat the oven to 350 degrees.

2 In a large bowl, cream the vegetable shortening and sugar until smooth. Beat in the egg yolks. Beat in the hard boiled egg yolks one at a time, beating well after each addition. Beat in the lemon zest. Gradually blend in the flour.

3 In a medium bowl, beat the egg white until stiff but not dry.

4 Break off small pieces of dough and form into crescent shapes. Dip in the beaten egg white and place 1 inch apart on ungreased baking sheets. (See Baking notes).

5 Sprinkle the cookies with the almonds and sugar. Bake for 10 to 12 minutes, until lightly colored. Transfer to wire racks to cool

Baking notes: If you prefer, place the cookies on the baking sheets and then brush with the beaten egg whites.

ALMOND TULIP PASTRY CUPS

Drop Cookies
YIELD: *2 to 3 dozen*
TOTAL TIME: *60 minutes*

¼ cup vegetable shortening
½ cup powdered sugar
2 large egg whites
¾ teaspoon Amaretto
¼ cup all-purpose flour
⅓ cup almonds, ground fine

1 Preheat the oven to 425 degrees.

2 In a large bowl, cream the vegetable shortening and powdered sugar. Add the egg whites and Amaretto, beating until very smooth. Gradually blend in the flour. Fold in the almonds.

3 Drop 1½ teaspoonfuls of the batter 5 inches apart onto ungreased baking sheets. With the back of a spoon, spread into 4- to 5-inch rounds.

4 Bake for 5 to 6 minutes, or until the edges are lightly browned. Using a spatula, remove the cookies from the sheets and place each cookie over an upside-down cup or glass. (If they become too firm to shape, return briefly to the oven.) Let cool completely before removing.

Baking notes: These are very easy to overbake; watch them closely. The cups can be used to hold fresh fruit, custards, or mousses. Or make smaller cups and fill them with whipped cream and sprinkle with shaved chocolate. (Do not fill the cookies until just before serving.) In an airtight container, the cups will keep well in the freezer for up to 6 months.

AMERICAN OATMEAL CRISPS

Drop Cookies
YIELD: *2 to 3 dozen*
TOTAL TIME: *30 minutes*

1¼ cups all-purpose flour
½ teaspoon baking powder
½ teaspoon baking soda
½ teaspoon salt
1 cup vegetable shortening
¼ cup granulated sugar
1 cup packed light brown sugar
2 large eggs
¼ cup milk
1 teaspoon almond extract
3 cups rolled oats
1 cup (6 ounces) baking chips (see Baking notes)

1 Preheat the oven to 350 degrees.

2 Combine the flour, baking powder, baking soda, and salt.

3 In a large bowl, cream the vegetable shortening and both sugars. Beat in the eggs. Beat in the milk and almond extract. Gradually blend in the dry ingredients. Fold in the oats and chips.

4 Drop the dough by teaspoonfuls about 1½ inches apart onto ungreased baking sheets.

5 Bake for 10 to 12 minutes, until golden brown. Transfer to wire racks to cool.

Baking notes: The baking chips can be semisweet, milk chocolate, white chocolate, peanut butter or butterscotch. For a cookie the children will love, omit the baking chips and press 4 or 5 M & M's into the top of each cookie.

AMERICAN SHORTBREAD

Rolled Cookies

YIELD: *8 dozen*
TOTAL TIME: *30 minutes*

2 cups (1 pound) butter, at room
   temperature
1¾ cups granulated sugar
6 large eggs
1 tablespoon caraway seeds
8 cups all-purpose flour

1 Preheat the oven to 400
degrees.

2 In a large bowl, cream the butter and sugar until light and
fluffy.

3 In another bowl, beat the eggs
until thick and light-colored. Beat
the eggs into the butter mixture.
Stir in the caraway seeds. Gradually blend in the flour.

4 On a floured surface, roll out
the dough ¼ inch thick. Cut into
1-inch squares and place 1 inch
apart on ungreased baking
sheets.

5 Bake for 12 to 15 minutes, until
lightly colored. Transfer to wire
racks to cool

Baking notes: For variation, substitute anise seeds for the caraway seeds. For variety, cut half
of the cookies into squares and
half into rounds with a cookie
cutter.

ANISE COOKIES

Drop Cookies

YIELD: *2 to 3 dozen*
TOTAL TIME: *30 minutes*
CHILLING TIME: *8 hours*

2¼ cups all-purpose flour
½ teaspoon baking powder
¼ teaspoon salt
2 large eggs
1½ cups granulated sugar
2 teaspoons anise extract

1 Combine the flour, baking
powder, and salt.

2 In a large bowl, beat the eggs
until foamy. Beat in the sugar
and anise extract. Gradually
blend in the dry ingredients.
Cover and chill for at least 8
hours, or overnight.

3 Preheat the oven to 325
degrees. Grease 2 baking sheets.

4 Drop the dough by spoonfuls
1½ inches apart onto the prepared baking sheets.

5 Bake for 10 to 12 minutes, until
lightly colored. Transfer to wire
racks to cool.

Baking notes: For a more subtle
flavor, substitute 2 teaspoons of
anise seeds for the anise extract.

Apple Cookies

Drop Cookies
YIELD: *3 to 4 dozen*
TOTAL TIME: *35 minutes*

2 cups all-purpose flour
1 teaspoon baking powder
½ teaspoon ground nutmeg
1 teaspoon ground cinnamon
½ teaspoon ground cloves
½ teaspoon salt
½ cup butter, at room temperature
1½ cups packed light brown sugar
1 large egg
¼ cup fresh lemon juice
1 teaspoon vanilla extract
1 cup diced, peeled apples
1 cup walnuts, chopped
1 cup raisins

GLAZE
1½ cups powdered sugar
1 tablespoon butter, at room
    temperature
2½ tablespoons evaporated milk
¼ teaspoon vanilla extract
Pinch of salt

1 Preheat the oven to 400 degrees. Grease 2 baking sheets.

2 Combine the flour, baking powder, spices, and salt.

3 In a large bowl, cream the butter and brown sugar. Beat in the egg, lemon juice, and vanilla extract. Gradually blend in the dry ingredients. Fold in the apples, walnuts, and raisins.

4 Drop the dough by teaspoonfuls 1½ inches apart onto the prepared baking sheets. Bake for 12 to 15 minutes, or until golden.

5 Meanwhile, make the glaze: Combine all the ingredients in a small bowl and beat until smooth.

6 Transfer the cookies to wire racks. Spread the glaze over the tops of the warm cookies, and let cool.

Apple-Raisin Drops

Drop Cookies
YIELD: *3 to 4 dozen*
TOTAL TIME: *35 minutes*

2 cups all-purpose flour
1 teaspoon baking powder
1 teaspoon ground cinnamon
½ teaspoon ground nutmeg
¼ teaspoon ground cloves
½ teaspoon salt
½ cup vegetable shortening
1 cup packed light brown sugar
2 large eggs
¼ cup milk
1½ cups diced, peeled apples
1 cup golden raisins
½ cup walnuts, chopped

1 Preheat the oven to 350 degrees. Grease 2 baking sheets.

2 Combine the flour, baking powder, spices, and salt.

3 In a large bowl, cream the vegetable shortening and brown sugar. Beat in the eggs and milk. Gradually blend in the dry ingredients. Fold in the apples, raisins and walnuts.

4 Drop the dough by spoonfuls 1½ inches apart onto the prepared baking sheets.

5 Bake for 12 to 14 minutes, or until lightly colored. Transfer to wire racks to cool.

APPLESAUCE COOKIES

Drop Cookies
YIELD: *5 to 6 dozen*
TOTAL TIME: *35 minutes*

1 cup golden raisins
About ⅓ cup brandy
1 package spice cake mix
½ cup canola oil
½ cup unsweetened applesauce
1 large egg

1 Preheat the oven to 350 degrees.

2 Place the raisins in a small bowl and add enough brandy to just cover. Set aside to plump for 10 minutes.

3 Prepare the cake mix according to the package directions, adding the oil, applesauce, and egg. Drain the raisins and fold them into the dough.

4 Drop the dough by spoonfuls 2 inches apart onto ungreased baking sheets.

5 Bake for 12 to 15 minutes, or until golden. Transfer to wire racks to cool.

APPLESAUCE DATE BARS

Bar Cookies
YIELD: *2 to 3 dozen*
TOTAL TIME: *45 minutes*

2 cups all-purpose flour
1 teaspoon ground cinnamon
½ teaspoon ground cardamom
Pinch of salt
¾ cup vegetable shortening
1 cup granulated sugar
2 teaspoons baking soda
1 tablespoon warm water
2 large eggs
2 cups unsweetened applesauce
1 cup pitted dates, chopped
1 cup walnuts, chopped

1 Preheat the oven to 350 degrees. Grease a 13 by 9-inch baking pan.

2 Combine the flour, cinnamon, cardamom, and salt.

3 In a large bowl, cream the vegetable shortening and sugar.

4 Dissolve the baking soda in the warm water and add to the creamed mixture, beating until smooth. Beat in the eggs. Beat in the applesauce. Gradually blend in the dry ingredients. Fold in the dates and walnuts.

5 Spread the mixture evenly in the prepared pan.

6 Bake for 25 to 30 minutes, or until golden brown on top. Cool in the pan on a rack before cutting into large or small bars.

Baking notes: For a decorative touch, frost these with Vanilla Icing (see Pantry), and drizzle Dark Chocolate Icing (see Pantry) over the top.

APRICOT CRESCENTS

Rolled Cookies

YIELD: *3 dozen*
TOTAL TIME: *40 minutes*
CHILLING TIME: *4 hours*

2 cups all-purpose flour
1 teaspoon granulated sugar
Pinch of salt
1 cup vegetable shortening
1 cup sour cream
1 large egg
½ cup apricot preserves
½ cup walnuts, chopped
Powdered sugar for dusting

1 Combine the flour, sugar, and salt in a bowl. Cut in the vegetable shortening until the mixture resembles coarse crumbs. With a fork stir in the sour cream and egg until a stiff dough forms. Cover and chill for at least 4 hours, or overnight.

2 Preheat the oven to 350 degrees. Grease 2 baking sheets.

3 Divide the dough into 3 pieces. On a floured surface, roll out each piece to an 11-inch round. Spread one-third of the apricot preserves evenly over each round, and sprinkle each round with one-third of the walnuts.

4 Cut each round into 12 wedges. Starting at the wide end, roll up each wedge. Place seam side down on the prepared baking sheets, placing the cookies about 1 inch apart and curving the ends to form crescent shapes.

5 Bake for 25 to 30 minutes, until lightly colored. Dust the warm cookies with powdered sugar and transfer to wire racks to cool.

APRICOT-SPICE COOKIES

Drop Cookies

YIELD: *2 to 3 dozen*
TOTAL TIME: *35 minutes*

1 cup dried apricots
2 cups all-purpose flour
1 teaspoon baking powder
1 teaspoon ground allspice
½ teaspoon ground cinnamon
½ teaspoon salt
½ cup vegetable shortening
1 cup granulated sugar
1 teaspoon baking soda
1 tablespoon warm water
1 large egg
1 cup golden raisins
1 cup pecans, chopped

1 Put the apricots through a food grinder, or grind them in a food processor or blender.

2 Combine the flour, baking powder, spices, and salt.

3 In a large bowl, cream the vegetable shortening and sugar.

4 Dissolve the baking soda in the warm water and add to the creamed mixture, beating until smooth. Beat in the egg. Gradually blend in the dry ingredients. Fold in the apricots, raisins, and pecans. Cover and chill for at least 1 hour.

5 Preheat the oven to 375 degrees. Grease 2 baking sheets.

6 Drop the dough by spoonfuls 1½ inches apart onto the prepared baking sheets.

7 Bake for 18 to 20 minutes, until browned on top. Transfer to wire racks to cool.

Arrowroot Biscuits

Drop Cookies

Yield: *3 to 4 dozen*
Total time: *30 minutes*

1½ cups all-purpose flour
½ cup arrowroot flour
¼ cup vegetable shortening
½ cup granulated sugar
2 large eggs
Granulated sugar for sprinkling

1 Preheat the oven to 350 degrees.

2 Sift together the all-purpose flour and arrowroot flour.

3 In a large bowl, cream the vegetable shortening and sugar until light and fluffy.

4 In another bowl, beat the eggs until thick and light-colored. Beat the eggs into the shortening. Fold in the flours.

5 Drop the dough by spoonfuls 1½ inches apart onto ungreased baking sheets.

6 Bake for 12 to 15 minutes, until lightly colored. Sprinkle the warm cookies with sugar and transfer to wire racks to cool.

Baking notes: Finely ground nuts, such as walnuts or almonds, can be added to the dough.

Aunt Lizzie's Cookies

Drop Cookies

Yield: *5 to 6 dozen*
Total time: *30 minutes*

3 cups all-purpose flour
1 teaspoon baking powder
1 cup vegetable shortening
1½ cups granulated sugar
3 large eggs
1 teaspoon vanilla extract
1 teaspoon baking soda
2 tablespoons hot water
1 cup walnuts, chopped
1 cup raisins

1 Preheat the oven to 325 degrees. Grease 2 baking sheets.

2 Combine the flour and baking powder.

3 In a large bowl, cream the vegetable shortening and sugar until light and fluffy.

4 In another bowl, beat the eggs until thick and light-colored. Beat the eggs into the shortening mixture. Beat in the vanilla extract.

5 Dissolve the baking soda in the hot water and add to the egg mixture, beating until smooth. Gradually blend in the dry ingredients. Fold in the walnuts and raisins.

6 Drop the dough by spoonfuls 1½ inches apart onto the prepared baking sheets.

7 Bake for 10 to 12 minutes, until lightly colored. Transfer to wire racks to cool.

Baking notes: According to my father, this recipe is of Swedish origin.

Austrian Walnut Crescents

Formed Cookies

YIELD: *4 to 6 dozen*
TOTAL TIME: *40 minutes*
CHILLING TIME: *4 hours*

1 cup vegetable shortening
⅔ cup granulated sugar
2 teaspoons vanilla extract
2½ cups all-purpose flour
¼ cup walnuts, chopped
Powdered sugar for rolling

1 In a large bowl, cream the vegetable shortening and sugar. Beat in the vanilla extract. Gradually blend in the flour and nuts. Cover and chill for at least 4 hours.

2 Preheat the oven to 325 degrees.

3 Break off small pieces of the dough and form into crescent shapes, curving the ends. Place 1 inch apart on ungreased baking sheets.

4 Bake for 15 to 20 minutes, until the edges are a light brown. Transfer to wire racks to cool slightly.

5 Roll the warm cookies in powdered sugar to coat. Let cool on the racks.

Baking notes: To make hazelnut crescents, an elegant variation, substitute hazelnut extract for the vanilla extract and chopped hazelnuts for the walnuts.

Banana Drops

Drop Cookies

YIELD: *3 to 4 dozen*
TOTAL TIME: *35 minutes*

1½ cups all-purpose flour
1 cup granulated sugar
½ teaspoon baking soda
¾ teaspoon ground cinnamon
¼ teaspoon ground nutmeg
1 teaspoon salt
¾ cup vegetable shortening
1 large egg
2 to 3 large bananas, mashed
1¾ cup rolled oats
2 cups (12 ounces) semisweet chocolate chips

1 Preheat the oven to 400 degrees.

2 Sift the flour, sugar, baking soda, cinnamon, nutmeg, and salt into a large bowl. Cut in the vegetable shortening. Stir in the egg and bananas until smooth. Fold in the oats and chocolate chips.

3 Drop the dough by spoonfuls 1½ inches apart onto ungreased baking sheets.

4 Bake for 12 to 15 minutes, until lightly colored. Transfer to wire racks to cool.

Baking notes: Raisins may be added to the dough. The chips can be of any type: semisweet or milk chocolate, butterscotch, or peanut butter.

Banana-Nut Drops

Drop Cookies

Yield: *3 to 4 dozen*
Total time: *35 minutes*

2¼ cups all-purpose flour
2 teaspoons baking powder
½ teaspoon salt
⅓ cup vegetable shortening
1 cup granulated sugar
2 large eggs
½ teaspoon vanilla extract
¼ teaspoon lemon extract
2 to 3 large bananas, mashed
½ cup walnuts, ground fine

1 Preheat the oven to 350 degrees. Grease 2 baking sheets.

2 Combine the flour, baking powder, and salt.

3 In a large bowl, cream the vegetable shortening and sugar. Beat in the eggs, vanilla extract, and lemon extract. Beat in the bananas and ground walnuts. Gradually blend in the dry ingredients.

4 Drop the dough by spoonfuls 1½ inches apart onto the prepared baking sheets.

5 Bake for 12 to 15 minute, until lightly colored. Transfer to wire racks to cool.

Banana-Oatmeal Cookies I

Drop Cookies

Yield: *3 to 5 dozen*
Total time: *30 minutes*

1½ cups all-purpose flour
½ teaspoon baking soda
¾ teaspoon ground cinnamon
¼ teaspoon ground nutmeg
¼ teaspoon salt
¾ cup vegetable shortening
1 cup granulated sugar
1 large egg
2 to 3 large bananas, mashed
1¾ cups rolled oats
½ cup almonds, chopped fine

1 Preheat the oven to 400 degrees.

2 Combine the flour, baking soda, cinnamon, nutmeg, and salt.

3 In a large bowl, cream the vegetable shortening and sugar. Beat in the egg and bananas. Gradually blend in the dry ingredients. Fold in the oats and almonds.

4 Drop the dough by spoonfuls 1½ inches apart onto ungreased baking sheets.

5 Bake for 12 to 15 minutes, until lightly colored. Transfer to wire racks to cool.

Banana-Oatmeal Cookies II

Drop Cookies
YIELD: *1 to 2 dozen*
TOTAL TIME: *35 minutes*

1½ cups all-purpose flour
¾ teaspoon ground cinnamon
¼ teaspoon ground nutmeg
¾ cup vegetable shortening
1 cup granulated sugar
1 large egg
½ cup mashed bananas
½ teaspoon baking soda
1 tablespoon warm water
1 teaspoon fresh lemon juice
1½ cup rolled oats

1 Preheat the oven to 350 degrees. Grease 2 baking sheets.

2 Combine the flour, cinnamon, and nutmeg.

3 In a large bowl, cream the vegetable shortening and sugar. Beat in the egg and bananas.

4 Dissolve the baking soda in the warm water and add to the banana mixture, beating until smooth. Beat in the lemon juice. Gradually blend in the dry ingredients. Fold in the oats.

5 Drop the dough by spoonfuls 1½ inches apart onto the prepared baking sheets.

6 Bake for 10 to 12 minutes, until golden brown. Transfer to wire racks to cool.

Baking notes: Raisins are good in this recipe.

Bannocks

Rolled Cookies
YIELD: *4–6*
TOTAL TIME: *35 minutes*

1¼ cups rolled oats
¾ cup all-purpose flour
1 tablespoon granulated sugar
1 tablespoon baking powder
½ teaspoon salt
5 tablespoons vegetable shortening
2 to 3 tablespoons water, or more as needed

1 Preheat the oven to 350 degrees.

2 Combine the rolled oats, flour, sugar, baking powder, and salt in a bowl. Using your fingertips, work in the vegetable shortening until the mixture resembles coarse crumbs. Add just enough water to form the mixture into a smooth dough.

3 On a floured surface, roll out the dough ½ inch thick. Using a butter plate as a guide, cut out 6-inch circles and place 1 inch apart on ungreased baking sheets.

4 Bake for 18 to 20 minutes, until the Bannocks are slightly colored and firm to the touch. Transfer to wire racks to cool.

Baking notes: This is a very old Scottish recipe. Bannocks are usually served with jam or jelly.

Beaumont Inn Cookies

Drop Cookies

YIELD: *2 to 3 dozen*
TOTAL TIME: *30 minutes*

2½ cups all-purpose flour
1 teaspoon baking powder
2 tablespoons butter, at room
  temperature
1 cup granulated sugar
1 large egg
½ cup milk

1 Preheat the oven to 425 degrees. Grease 2 baking sheets.

2 Combine the flour and baking powder.

3 In a large bowl, cream the butter and sugar. Beat in the egg and milk. Gradually blend in the dry ingredients.

4 Drop the dough by spoonfuls 1½ inches apart onto the prepared baking sheets.

5 Bake for 12 to 15 minutes, until golden brown. Transfer to wire racks to cool.

Baking notes: The Beaumont Inn is located in Harrodsburg, Kentucky. These cookies can be decorated with raisins, slivered nuts, or glacé cherries before baking.

Benne (Sesame Seed) Cookies

Drop Cookies

YIELD: *3 to 4 dozen*
TOTAL TIME: *30 minutes*

1¼ cups all-purpose flour
¼ teaspoon baking powder
¼ teaspoon salt
¾ cup butter, at room temperature
1½ cups packed light brown sugar
2 large eggs
1 teaspoon vanilla extract
½ cup sesame seeds, toasted

1 Preheat the oven to 350 degrees. Grease 2 baking sheets.

2 Combine the flour, baking powder, and salt.

3 In a large bowl, cream the butter and sugar. Beat in the eggs and vanilla extract. Gradually blend in the dry ingredients. Fold in the sesame seeds.

4 Drop the dough by spoonfuls 1½ inches apart onto the prepared baking sheets.

5 Bake for 10 to 12 minutes, until lightly colored. Transfer to wire racks to cool.

Baking notes: These cookies are an old Southern favorite. Sesame seeds are called "Benne seeds" in the South.

Berlin Garlands

Rolled Cookies

YIELD: *4 to 5 dozen*
TOTAL TIME: *35 minutes*
CHILLING TIME: *8 hours*

2 large egg yolks
2 hard-boiled large eggs, coarsely chopped
1½ cups powdered sugar
¾ cup butter, at room temperature
2 cups all-purpose flour
2 large egg whites
Powdered sugar for sprinkling

1 In a large bowl, combine the egg yolks and hard-boiled eggs and beat until thick and light-colored. Beat in the sugar. Beat in the butter. Gradually blend in the flour. Cover and chill for 8 hours.

2 Preheat the oven to 350 degrees. Grease 2 baking sheets.

3 On a floured surface, roll out the dough ½ inch thick. Cut into pencil-thin strips 6 to 8 inches long.

4 For each cookie, braid 3 strips together, shape into a circle and pinch the ends to seal. Place the cookies 1 inch apart on the prepared baking sheets.

5 In a large bowl, beat the egg whites until they hold stiff peaks. Brush the cookies with the beaten egg whites and sprinkle with powdered sugar.

6 Bake for 12 to 15 minutes, until lightly colored. Transfer to wire racks to cool.

Baking notes: It is important to allow the batter to sit for 8 hours or overnight. The strips should be about the size of a pencil. I also like to combine finely chopped hazelnuts with the powdered sugar for sprinkling.

Billy Goats

Drop Cookies

YIELD: *5 to 6 dozen*
TOTAL TIME: *30 minutes*

4 cups all-purpose flour
1 tablespoon plus 1 teaspoon baking powder
1 teaspoon ground allspice
1 cup walnuts, chopped
½ teaspoon salt
1 cup vegetable shortening
2 cups granulated sugar
4 large eggs
1 teaspoon vanilla extract
1 teaspoon baking soda
1 tablespoon warm water
1 cup sour cream
1½ cups dates, pitted and chopped

1 Preheat the oven to 350 degrees. Grease 2 baking sheets.

2 Combine the flour, baking powder, allspice, and salt.

3 In a large bowl, cream the vegetable shortening and sugar. Beat in the eggs one at a time. Beat in the vanilla extract.

4 Dissolve the baking soda in the warm water and add to the egg mixture, beating until smooth. Beat in the sour cream. Gradually blend in the dry ingredients. Fold in the dates and walnuts.

5 Drop the dough by spoonfuls 1½ inches apart onto the prepared baking sheets.

6 Bake for 12 to 15 minutes, until golden. Transfer to wire racks to cool.

Baking notes: Raisins may be substituted for the dates; plump them in warm water before using. For a slightly different flavor, ground nutmeg may be used in place of the allspice.

BIRD'S NEST COOKIES

Formed Cookies

YIELD: *3 to 4 dozen*
TOTAL TIME: *35 minutes*

2 cups all-purpose flour
¼ teaspoon salt
1 cup vegetable shortening
½ cup granulated sugar
1 large egg, separated
1 large egg yolk
1½ teaspoons vanilla extract
1 cup walnuts, chopped
Chocolate kisses for garnish

1 Preheat the oven to 375 degrees.

2 Combine the flour and salt.

3 In a large bowl, cream the vegetable shortening and sugar. Beat in the egg yolks and vanilla extract. Gradually blend in the dry ingredients.

4 In a shallow bowl, beat the egg white until frothy. Spread the walnuts on waxed paper.

5 Break off 1-inch pieces of dough and roll into balls. Dip the balls in the egg white to coat, then roll in the walnuts and place 1 inch apart on ungreased baking sheets.

6 With your finger, make a small depression in the center of each cookie. Bake for 12 to 15 minutes, until lightly colored.

7 Press an upside-down chocolate kiss into the center of each hot cookie, and transfer to wire racks to cool.

BISCOTTI

Rolled Cookies

YIELD: *3 to 4 dozen*
TOTAL TIME: *30 minutes*

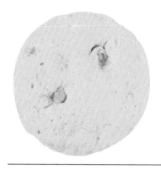

2 cups all-purpose flour
½ cup granulated sugar
½ teaspoon baking powder
6 tablespoons vegetable shortening
4 large eggs
½ cup walnuts, chopped

1 Preheat the oven to 350 degrees. Grease 2 baking sheets.

2 In a medium bowl, combine the flour, sugar, and baking powder. Cut in the vegetable shortening until the mixture resembles coarse crumbs.

3 In a large bowl, beat the eggs until thick and light-colored. Gradually beat the eggs into the flour mixture. Fold in the walnuts.

4 On a floured surface, roll out the dough ¼ inch thick. Using a cookie cutter, cut into shapes and place 1½ inches apart on the prepared baking sheets.

5 Bake for 12 to 14 minutes, until lightly colored. Transfer to wire racks to cool.

BISHOP'S PEPPER COOKIES

Rolled Cookies

YIELD: *3 to 4 dozen*
TOTAL TIME: *30 minutes*
CHILLING TIME: *4 hours*

2½ cups all-purpose flour
¼ cup almonds, ground fine
½ teaspoon baking soda
1 teaspoon ground cinnamon
1 teaspoon ground ginger
½ teaspoon ground allspice
½ teaspoon salt
1 cup vegetable shortening
1 cup granulated sugar
½ cup corn syrup
1 large egg

1 Combine the flour, almonds, baking soda, spices, and salt.

2 In a large bowl, cream the vegetable shortening and sugar. Beat in the corn syrup. Beat in the egg. Gradually blend in the dry ingredients. Cover and chill for at least 4 hours.

3 Preheat the oven to 350 degrees.

4 On a floured surface, roll out the dough ¼ inch thick. Using cookie cutters, cut out shapes and place 1½ inches apart on ungreased baking sheets.

5 Bake for 8 to 10 minutes, until lightly colored. Transfer to wire racks to cool.

Baking notes: These cookies are traditionally decorated with Royal Icing (see Pantry) piped in various designs over the top.

BLACKBERRY COOKIES

Drop Cookies

YIELD: *4 to 5 dozen*
TOTAL TIME: *30 minutes*
CHILLING TIME: *4 hours*

2 cups all-purpose flour
2 teaspoons baking powder
½ teaspoon salt
½ cup vegetable shortening
1 cup granulated sugar
1 large egg
¼ cup milk
1½ teaspoons grated lemon zest
1 cup blackberry puree, unstrained

1 Combine the flour, baking powder, and salt.

2 In a large bowl, cream the vegetable shortening and sugar. Beat in the egg and milk. Beat in the lemon zest. Gradually blend in the dry ingredients. Fold in the blackberry puree. Cover and chill for at least 4 hours.

3 Preheat the oven to 375 degrees.

4 Drop the dough by spoonfuls 1½ inches apart onto ungreased baking sheets.

5 Bake for 12 to 15 minutes, until lightly colored. Transfer to wire racks to cool.

Baking notes: You can make these with fresh blackberries instead of the puree. Rinse and thoroughly dry fresh berries. Add the berries to the flour mixture, tossing them gently to coat thoroughly.

Black Walnut Refrigerator Cookies

Refrigerator Cookies
Yield: 8 to 9 dozen
Total time: 30 minutes
Chilling time: 24 hours

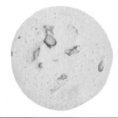

Blueberry Cookies

Drop Cookies
Yield: 4 to 5 dozen
Total time: 30 minutes
Chilling time: 4 hours

2⅔ cups all-purpose flour
2 teaspoons baking powder
¼ teaspoon salt
¾ cup butter, at room temperature
1½ cups packed light brown sugar
2 large eggs
1 teaspoon vanilla extract
1½ cups black walnuts, chopped

1 Combine the flour, baking powder, and salt.

2 In a large bowl, cream the butter and brown sugar. Beat in the eggs and vanilla extract. Gradually blend in the dry ingredients. Fold in the walnuts. Cover and refrigerate just until firm enough to shape, about 30 minutes.

3 Divide the dough into 3 pieces. Form each piece into a log about 8 inches long. Wrap in waxed paper and chill for at least 24 hours.

4 Preheat the oven to 375 degrees. Grease 2 baking sheets.

5 Slice the logs into ¼-inch-thick slices and place 1 inch apart on the prepared baking sheets.

6 Bake for 8 to 10 minutes, until lightly colored. Transfer to wire racks to cool.

2 cups all-purpose flour
2 teaspoons baking powder
½ teaspoon salt
½ cup vegetable shortening
1 cup granulated sugar
1 large egg
¼ cup milk
1 teaspoon almond extract
1½ teaspoons grated lemon zest
1 cup blueberries

1 Combine the flour, baking powder, and salt.

2 In a large bowl, cream the vegetable shortening and sugar. Beat in the egg. Beat in the milk, almond extract, and lemon zest. Gradually blend in the dry ingredients. Fold in the blueberries.

3 Cover and chill for at least 4 hours.

4 Preheat the oven to 375 degrees.

5 Drop the dough by spoonfuls about 1 inch apart onto ungreased baking sheets.

6 Bake for 12 to 15 minutes, until lightly colored. Transfer to wire racks to cool

Baking notes: Canned or frozen blueberries can be used, but fresh give the best results.

BLUSHING COOKIES

Rolled Cookies

YIELD: *2 to 3 dozen*
TOTAL TIME: *30 minutes*

2 cups all-purpose flour
1 cup walnuts, chopped fine
¼ teaspoon ground cinnamon
½ cup vegetable shortening
¾ cup powdered sugar
Red jimmies for sprinkling

1 Preheat the oven to 400 degrees.

2 Combine the flour, walnuts, and cinnamon.

3 In a large bowl, cream the vegetable shortening and powdered sugar until light and fluffy. Gradually blend in the dry ingredients.

4 On a floured surface, roll out the dough ¼ inch thick. Using cookie cutter, cut into shapes and place on ungreased baking sheets. Sprinkle the rainbow jimmies over the tops of the cookies.

5 Bake for 8 to 10 minutes, until lightly colored. Transfer to wire racks to cool.

BOURBON BALLS

Formed Cookies

YIELD: *3 to 5 dozen*
TOTAL TIME: *30 minutes*

2½ cups crushed vanilla wafers
1 cup walnuts, ground fine
¾ cup semisweet chocolate chips
½ cup granulated sugar
2 tablespoons corn syrup
½ cup bourbon
Powdered sugar for rolling

1 Combine the vanilla wafers and walnuts.

2 Melt the chocolate chips in a double boiler over low heat, stirring until smooth. Stir in the sugar and corn syrup. Remove from the heat and stir in the bourbon. Add the vanilla wafer mixture all at once and blend to form a thick dough.

3 Break off pieces of dough and form into balls. Roll each ball in powdered sugar. Store in an airtight container until ready to serve.

Baking notes: Almost any type of whiskey can be substituted for the bourbon. Obviously, these cookies are not for children.

BONBONS

Formed Cookies

YIELD: *3 dozen*
TOTAL TIME: *40 minutes*

1½ cups all-purpose flour
½ teaspoon salt
½ cup vegetable shortening
½ cups powdered sugar
2 tablespoons heavy cream
2 teaspoons vanilla extract
36 candied glacé cherries

1 Preheat the oven to 350 degrees.

2 Combine the flour and salt.

3 In a large bowl, cream the vegetable shortening and powdered sugar. Beat in the cream and vanilla extract. Gradually blend in the dry ingredients.

4 Break off pieces of dough and flatten each one on a floured surface into a round about 3 to 4 inches in diameter. Place a candied cherry in the center of each round and wrap the dough up around the cherry. Pinch to seal. Place 1 inch apart on ungreased baking sheets.

5 Bake for 8 to 10 minutes, until the dough is set (see Baking notes). Transfer to wire racks to cool.

Baking notes: It is important not to overbake these cookies; bake only until the dough is set. Do not let it color at all. To decorate, dip the top of each ball into sugar icing or melted chocolate. To completely coat the cookies with chocolate, place the cookies one at a time on a bamboo skewer and dip in melted chocolate. Hold the skewer at an angle so cookie does not slip off it. For an unusual variation, add 3 tablespoons of unsweetened cocoa powder to the dough, and dip the tops of the baked bonbons in melted white chocolate.

Bourbon Chews

Drop Cookies

Yield: *3 to 4 dozen*
Total time: *30 minutes*

1 cup all-purpose flour
1 teaspoon ground ginger
½ teaspoon salt
½ cup vegetable shortening
¼ cup molasses
2 tablespoons bourbon
½ cup packed light brown sugar
¼ cup walnuts, chopped

1 Preheat the oven to 325 degrees. Lightly grease 2 baking sheets.

2 Combine the flour, ginger, and salt together.

3 In a small saucepan combine the molasses and vegetable shortening and heat over low heat, stirring until smooth. Remove from the heat and add the bourbon. Beat in the brown sugar. Gradually blend in the dry ingredients. Fold in the walnuts.

4 Drop the dough by spoonfuls onto the prepared baking sheets.

5 Bake for 10 to 12 minutes, until lightly colored. Transfer to wire racks to cool.

Boysenberry Cookies

Drop Cookies

Yield: *4 to 5 dozen*
Total time: *30 minutes*
Chilling time: *4 hours*

2 cups all-purpose flour
2 teaspoons baking powder
½ teaspoon salt
½ cup vegetable shortening
1 cup granulated sugar
1 large egg
¼ cup milk
1½ teaspoons grated lemon zest
1 cup boysenberries, crushed and strained to remove the seeds

1 Combine the flour, baking powder and salt.

2 In a large bowl, cream the vegetable shortening and sugar. Beat in the egg. Beat in the milk and lemon zest. Gradually blend in the dry ingredients. Blend in the boysenberries. Cover and chill for at least 4 hours.

3 Preheat the oven to 375 degrees.

4 Drop the dough by spoonfuls about 1 inch apart onto ungreased baking sheets.

5 Bake for 12 to 15 minutes, until golden. Transfer to wire racks to cool.

Brandy Cookies

Formed Cookies

Yield: *1 to 3 dozen*
Total time: *30 minutes*

1 cup vegetable shortening
½ cup granulated sugar
1 tablespoon brandy
¼ cup unsweetened cocoa powder
3 cups all-purpose flour

1 Preheat the oven to 350 degrees.

2 In large bowl, cream the vegetable shortening and sugar. Beat in the brandy. Blend in the cocoa powder. Gradually blend in the flour.

3 Place the dough in a cookie press or a pastry bag fitted with a plain round tip. Press or pipe the dough onto ungreased baking sheets, spacing the cookies 1½ inches apart.

4 Bake for 8 to 10 minutes, until light golden. Transfer to wire racks to cool.

Baking notes: These cookies are usually formed using a plain round tip, but you can experiment with other shapes. This dough keeps well in the rerigerator; it also freezes well. It can also be rolled out ¼ inch thick and cut into shapes with cookie cutters. For variation, use candied fruit to decorate the cookies.

Brazil-Nut Balls

Formed Cookies

Yield: *6 to 8 dozen*
Total time: *30 minutes*

2 cups all-purpose flour
½ teaspoon salt
¾ cup vegetable shortening
½ cup granulated sugar
1 large egg
2 cups brazil nuts, ground fine
Powdered sugar for rolling

1 Preheat the oven to 350 degrees.

2 Combine the flour and salt.

3 In a large bowl, cream the vegetable shortening and sugar. Beat in the egg. Gradually blend in the dry ingredients. Stir in the nuts.

4 Break off walnut-sized pieces of dough and form into balls. Roll in powered sugar and place 1 inch apart on ungreased baking sheets.

5 Bake for 15 to 20 minutes, until firm to the touch. Roll the hot cookies in powdered sugar and place on wire racks to cool. When cool roll in powdered sugar again.

Brazil-Nut Cookies

Drop Cookies

YIELD: *2 to 3 dozen*
TOTAL TIME: *30 minutes*
CHILLING TIME: *4 hours*

1¾ cups all-purpose flour
½ teaspoon salt
1 cup vegetable shortening
1 cup granulated sugar
1 large egg
1 teaspoon vanilla extract
1 cup brazil nuts, sliced thin
About 1½ cups whole brazil nuts

1 Combine the flour and salt.

2 In a large bowl, cream the vegetable shortening and sugar. Beat in the egg. Beat in the vanilla extract. Gradually blend in the dry ingredients. Fold in the sliced nuts. Cover and chill for at least 4 hours.

3 Preheat the oven to 375 degrees. Lightly grease 2 baking sheets.

4 Drop the dough by tablespoonfuls 1½ inches apart onto the prepared baking sheets. Press a whole brazil nut into each cookie.

5 Bake for 10 to 12 minutes, until golden brown. Transfer to wire racks to cool.

Brown Sugar Sand Tarts

Rolled Cookies

YIELD: *3 to 5 dozen*
TOTAL TIME: *30 minutes*
CHILLING TIME: *2 hours*

¾ cup all-purpose flour
¼ teaspoon baking powder
¼ teaspoon salt
¼ cup butter, at room temperature
⅓ cup packed light brown sugar
1 large egg
½ teaspoon vanilla extract
Light brown sugar for sprinkling

1 Combine the flour, baking powder, and salt.

2 In a large bowl, cream the butter and brown sugar. Beat in the egg. Beat in the vanilla extract. Gradually blend in the dry ingredients. Cover and chill for 2 hours.

3 Preheat the oven to 375 degrees. Lightly grease 2 baking sheets.

4 On a floured surface, roll out the dough to a thickness of ⅛ inch. With cookie cutters, cut into shapes and place 1 inch apart on the prepared baking sheets. Sprinkle with brown sugar and lightly press the sugar into the cookie.

5 Bake for 8 to 10 minutes, until firm to the touch. Transfer to wire racks to cool.

Brown-Eyed Susans

Formed Cookies

Yield: *4 to 5 dozen*
Total time: *30 minutes*
Chilling time: *1 hour*

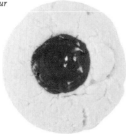

1¾ cups all-purpose flour
¼ teaspoon salt
¾ cup vegetable shortening
½ cup granulated sugar
1 large egg
1 teaspoon vanilla extract
7 ounces milk chocolate, chopped

1 Combine the flour and salt.

2 In a large bowl, cream the vegetable shortening and sugar. Beat in the egg. Beat in the vanilla extract. Gradually blend in the dry ingredients. Cover and chill for 1 hour.

3 Preheat the oven to 400 degrees.

4 Melt the milk chocolate in the top half of a double boiler over a low heat, stirring until smooth. Remove from the heat; keep warm over hot water.

5 Break off small pieces of the dough and roll into balls. Place 1½ inches apart on ungreased baking sheets. Press your finger into the center of each ball to make a slight indentation.

6 Bake for 8 to 10 minutes, until lightly colored. Spoon a little of the melted milk chocolate into the center of each hot cookie and transfer to wire racks to cool.

Baking notes: This dough can be frozen for up to a month. You can also shape the dough into balls and freeze until ready to bake; let stand for two hours at room temperature. Then bake according to the instructions above. Fill the centers of the cookies with jam or jelly instead of the milk chocolate. Or add 2 tablespoons unsweetened cocoa powder to the dough, and fill the baked cookies with melted white chocolate.

Butter Cookies I

Rolled Cookies

YIELD: *2 to 3 dozen*
TOTAL TIME: *30 minutes*
CHILLING TIME: *12 hours*

1 cup butter, at room temperature
½ cup granulated sugar
1 large egg yolk
½ teaspoon almond extract
2⅓ cups all-purpose flour
½ cup almonds, ground fine
1 large egg white, lightly beaten
Jam or preserves for filling

1 In a large bowl, cream the butter and sugar. Beat in the egg yolk. Beat in the almond extract. Gradually blend in the flour. Cover and chill for 12 hours.

2 Preheat the oven to 350 degrees.

3 On a floured surface, roll out the dough to a thickness of ¼ inch. Using a 2-inch round cookie cutter, cut into circles. Using a ½-inch round cookie cutter, cut out the centers of one half of the cookies. Place the cookies 1½ inches apart on ungreased baking sheets. Brush the cut-out cookies with beaten egg white and sprinkle the ground almonds over the top.

4 Bake for 8 to 10 minutes, until lightly colored. Transfer to wire racks to cool.

5 Spread a layer of jam or preserves over the plain cookies and top with the cut-out cookies.

Baking notes: Jelly does not usually make a good filling for cookies because it is too thin. Use any small cookie cutter to make the center cut-out: angels, dogs, cats, Santa's, etc.

Butter Cookies II

Rolled Cookies

YIELD: *6 to 8 dozen*
TOTAL TIME: *30 minutes*

1 cup butter
4 cups all-purpose flour
3 large eggs
2 cups granulated sugar

1 Preheat the oven to 350 degrees.

2 Melt the butter in a large saucepan. Remove from heat and add 2 cups of the flour all at once. Beat in the eggs one at a time. Beat in the sugar. Gradually blend in the remaining flour.

3 On a floured surface, roll out the dough to a thickness of ¼ inch. Using cookie cutters, cut into shapes and place the cookies 1½ inches apart on ungreased baking sheets.

4 Bake for 12 to 15 minutes, until lightly colored. Transfer to wire racks to cool.

Baking notes: For a different texture, substitute ½ cup rice flour for ½ cup of the all-purpose flour.

Butter Cookies III

Rolled Cookies

Yield: *6 to 10 dozen*
Total time: *30 minutes*

2 cups butter, at room temperature
1 cup powdered sugar
2 large eggs
4 cups all-purpose flour

1 Preheat the oven to 350 degrees.

2 In a large bowl, cream the butter and powdered sugar. Beat in the eggs one at a time. Gradually blend in the flour.

3 On a floured surface, roll out the dough to a thickness of ¼ inch. With a 1½-inch round cookie cutter, cut out circles and place them 1 inch apart on ungreased baking sheets.

4 Bake for 12 to 15 minutes, until lightly colored. Transfer to wire racks to cool.

Buttermilk Cookies

Rolled Cookies

Yield: *3 to 4 dozen*
Total time: *30 minutes*
Chilling time: *8 hours*

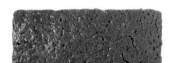

3½ cups all-purpose flour
1 teaspoon baking soda
1 teaspoon ground nutmeg
⅛ teaspoon salt
1 cup vegetable shortening
1 cup granulated sugar
1 large egg
½ cup buttermilk

1 Combine the flour, baking soda, nutmeg, and salt.

2 In a large bowl, cream the vegetable shortening and sugar. Beat in the egg. Beat in the buttermilk. Gradually blend in the dry ingredients. Cover and chill for 8 hours or overnight.

3 Preheat the oven to 350 degrees.

4 On a floured surface, roll out the dough to a thickness of ¼ inch. Using cookie cutters, cut into shapes and place 1½ inches apart on ungreased baking sheets.

5 Bake for 10 to 12 minutes, until lightly colored. Transfer to wire racks to cool.

BUTTERNUT DROPS

Formed Cookies

YIELD: *4 to 6 dozen*
TOTAL TIME: *30 minutes*
CHILLING TIME: *4 hours*

½ cup vegetable shortening
¼ cup granulated sugar
1 large egg
1 teaspoon vanilla extract
1 tablespoon fresh lemon juice
2 tablespoons grated orange zest
1 tablespoon grated lemon zest
1 cup all-purpose flour
1 egg white
½ cup brazil nuts, chopped
Candied cherries for garnish

1 In a large bowl, cream the vegetable shortening and sugar. Beat in the egg. Beat in the vanilla extract and lemon juice. Beat in the orange and lemon zest. Gradually blend in the flour. Cover and chill for 4 hours.

2 Preheat the oven to 350 degrees.

3 In a small bowl, beat the egg white until stiff but not dry. Spread the chopped nuts on a plate.

4 Break off small pieces of dough and form into balls. Roll each ball in the beaten egg white, then in the brazil nuts, and place 1½ inches apart on ungreased baking sheets. Press a candied cherry into the center of each ball.

5 Bake for 12 to 15 minutes, or until golden brown. Transfer to wire racks to cool.

BUTTERSCOTCH COOKIES

Drop Cookies

YIELD: *3 to 5 dozen*
TOTAL TIME: *30 minutes*

2 cups all-purpose flour
½ teaspoon baking soda
½ teaspoon salt
¾ cup vegetable shortening
1 cup packed light brown sugar
2 large eggs
1 cup (6 ounces) rolled oats
½ cup almonds, chopped
1 cup butterscotch chips

1 Preheat the oven to 350 degrees. Lightly grease 2 baking sheets.

2 Combine the flour, baking soda, and salt.

3 In a large bowl, cream the vegetable shortening and brown sugar. Beat in the eggs. Gradually blend in the dry ingredients. Fold in the oats and almonds. Fold in the butterscotch chips.

4 Drop the dough by spoonfuls 2 inches apart onto the prepared baking sheets.

5 Bake for 10 to 12 minutes, until lightly browned. Transfer to wire racks to cool.

Butterscotch Chocolate Pinwheels

Refrigerator Cookies

Yield: *4 to 6 dozen*
Total time: *30 minutes*
Chilling time: *2*

Butterscotch Dough
1½ cups all-purpose flour
½ teaspoon baking soda
¼ teaspoon salt
½ cup butter, at room temperature
1 cup packed light brown sugar
1 large egg
1 teaspoon vanilla extract

Chocolate Dough
1 cup all-purpose flour
½ cup rice flour
1 tablespoon unsweetened cocoa powder
½ teaspoon baking soda
¼ teaspoon salt
½ cup vegetable shortening
1 cup granulated sugar
1 large egg
1 teaspoon vanilla extract

1 To make the butterscotch dough, combine the flour, baking soda, and salt.

2 In a large bowl, cream the butter and brown sugar. Beat in the egg and vanilla extract. Gradually blend in the dry ingredients. Divide the dough in half. Wrap each half in waxed paper and chill for 2 hours.

3 Meanwhile, make the chocolate dough: Combine the flour, rice flour, cocoa powder, baking soda, and salt.

4 In a large bowl, cream the vegetable shortening and sugar. Beat in the egg and vanilla extract. Gradually blend in the dry ingredients. Divide the dough in half. Wrap each half in waxed paper and chill for 2 hours.

5 On a floured surface, roll out half the butterscotch dough to a 10 by 8-inch rectangle. Roll out half the chocolate dough to the same size. Brush the top of the butterscotch dough lightly with water and place the chocolate square on top. Starting at a long end, roll up jelly-roll fashion, and pinch the seam to seal. Wrap in waxed paper and chill for 24 hours. Repeat with the remaining dough.

6 Preheat the oven to 375 degrees. Lightly grease 2 baking sheets.

7 Slice the rolls into ¼-inch-thick-slices and place 1½ inches apart on the prepared baking sheets.

8 Bake for 8 to 10 minutes, until lightly browned. Transfer to wire racks to cool.

Calla Lilies

Drop Cookies

YIELD: *2 to 3 dozen*
TOTAL TIME: *30 minutes*

1 cup all-purpose flour
1 teaspoon baking powder
⅛ teaspoon salt
3 large large egg whites
¾ cup granulated sugar
1 teaspoon vanilla extract

FILLING
½ cup heavy cream
2 tablespoons granulated sugar

1 Preheat the oven to 400 degrees. Lightly grease 2 baking sheets.

2 Combine the flour, baking powder, and salt.

3 In a large bowl, beat the egg whites until stiff but not dry. Beat in the sugar and vanilla extract. Gradually fold in the dry ingredients. Beat for 2 minutes.

4 Drop the dough by spoonfuls onto the prepared baking sheets.

5 Bake for 8 to 10 minutes, until golden. While the cookies are still hot, roll each one into a cone shape and place seam side down on wire racks to cool.

6 To prepare the filling, in a small bowl beat the heavy cream with the sugar until it holds soft peaks. Just before serving, fill the cones with the whipped cream

Baking notes: For variation, add diced fresh fruit to the whipped cream before filling the cones.

Candy Gumdrop Cookies

Formed Cookies

YIELD: *2 to 3 dozen*
TOTAL TIME: *30 minutes*

2 cups all-purpose flour
1 teaspoon baking soda
1 teaspoon salt
1 cup vegetable shortening
1 cup granulated sugar
1 cup packed light brown sugar
2 large eggs
1 teaspoon vanilla extract
2 cups rolled oats
1 cup shredded coconut
1 cup gumdrops, diced
Powdered sugar for rolling

1 Preheat the oven to 350 degrees. Lightly grease 2 baking sheets.

2 Combine the flour, baking soda and salt.

3 In a large bowl, cream the vegetable shortening and two sugars. Beat in the eggs one at a time. Beat in the vanilla extract. Gradually blend in the dry ingredients. Fold in the oats, coconut, and gumdrops.

4 Pinch off small pieces of the dough and form into balls. Place 1 inch apart on the prepared baking sheets.

5 Bake for 10 to 12 minutes, until firm to the touch. Transfer to wire racks to cool.

6 When the cookies are cool, roll them in powdered sugar.

Baking notes: For flat cookies, place the balls 1½ inches apart on the baking sheets and flatten them with the bottom of a glass dipped in flour.

CAROB CHIP OATMEAL COOKIES

Drop Cookies

YIELD: *2 to 3 dozen*
TOTAL TIME: *30 minutes*

2½ cup all-purpose flour
1 tablespoon baking soda
¼ teaspoon salt
1 cup vegetable shortening
¼ cup honey
2 large eggs
2 cups rolled oats
¾ cup carob chips
1 cup golden raisins
1 cup walnuts, chopped

1 Preheat the oven to 350 degrees. Lightly grease 2 baking sheets.

2 Combine the flour, baking soda, and salt.

3 In a large saucepan, melt the vegetable shortening with the honey, stirring until smooth. Remove from the heat and beat in the eggs one at a time. Gradually blend in the dry ingredients. Fold in the oats, carob chips, raisins, and walnuts.

4 Drop the dough by spoonfuls 1½ inches apart onto the prepared baking sheets.

5 Bake for 12 to 15 minutes, until golden brown. Transfer to wire racks to cool.

CASHEW COOKIES

Drop Cookies

YIELD: *3 to 5 dozen*
TOTAL TIME: *30 minutes*

⅓ cup all-purpose flour
⅓ cup rice flour
2 cups cashews, ground fine
¼ teaspoon baking soda
4 large eggs
1 tablespoon rum
Chopped cashews for topping

1 Preheat the oven to 350 degrees. Lightly grease 2 baking sheets.

2 Combine the two flours, the ground cashews, and baking soda.

3 In a large bowl, beat the eggs until light and foamy. Beat in the rum. Gradually blend in the dry ingredients.

4 Drop the cookies by spoonfuls 1½ inches apart onto the prepared baking sheets and sprinkle chopped cashews on top of the cookies.

5 Bake for 5 to 8 minutes, until lightly colored. Transfer to wire racks to cool.

CASHEW SHORTBREAD

Formed Cookies
YIELD: *4 to 5 dozen*
TOTAL TIME: *30 minutes*

4½ cups all-purpose flour
1 cup cashews, ground fine
2 cups vegetable shortening
2½ cups packed light brown sugar

1 Preheat the oven to 350 degrees.

2 Combine the flour and cashews.

3 In a large bowl, cream the vegetable shortening and brown sugar. Gradually blend in the dry ingredients.

4 Pinch off small pieces of dough and roll into a balls. Place 1 inch apart on ungreased baking sheets. Flatten the balls with the bottom of a glass dipped in flour.

5 Bake for 10 to 15 minutes, until lightly colored. Transfer to wire racks to cool.

CHERRY-ALMOND KOLACKY

Rolled Cookies
YIELD: *3 to 4 dozen*
TOTAL TIME: *35 minutes*
CHILLING TIME: *4 hours*

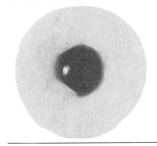

⅔ cup butter, at room temperature
¼ cup rice flour
½ teaspoon Amaretto
1 tablespoon plus 1 teaspoon orange liqueur
10 ounces cream cheese, at room temperature
2 cups all-purpose flour
Approximately 1 cup glacé cherries, cut in half

1 In a large bowl, beat the butter and rice flour until smooth. Beat in the Amaretto and 1 teaspoon of the orange liqueur. Beat in the cream cheese. Gradually blend in the all-purpose flour. Cover and chill for 4 hours.

2 Meanwhile, combine the cherries 1 cup warm water, and the remaining 1 tablespoon orange liqueur in a small bowl. Set aside and let plump for at least 1 hour.

3 Preheat the oven to 350 degrees.

4 Drain the cherries, discarding the liquid.

5 On a floured surface, roll out the dough to a thickness of ¼ inch. Using a 2- to 2½-inch round cookie cutter, cut into rounds and place 1 inch apart on ungreased baking sheets. Press a cherry half into the center of each cookie.

6 Bake for 10 to 15 minutes, until the edges are lighly colored. Transfer to wire racks to cool.

Baking notes: Use a combination of both red and green cherries if you like.

CHOCOLATE CHIP COOKIES I

Drop Cookies

YIELD: *6 to 7 dozen*
TOTAL TIME: *30 minutes*

2¼ cups all-purpose flour
1 teaspoon baking soda
1 package vanilla-flavored instant pudding
1 cup vegetable shortening
¼ cup granulated sugar
¾ cup packed light brown sugar
2 large eggs
1 teaspoon vanilla extract
1½ cups (9 ounces) semisweet chocolate chips
1 cup walnuts, chopped fine

1 Preheat the oven to 375 degrees.

2 Combine the flour, baking soda, and vanilla pudding

3 In a large bowl, cream the vegetable shortening and the two sugars. Beat in the eggs. Beat in the vanilla extract. Gradually blend in the dry ingredients. Fold in the chocolate chips and walnuts.

4 Drop the dough by spoonfuls 1½ inches apart onto ungreased baking sheets.

5 Bake for 8 to 10 minutes, until lightly colored. Transfer to wire racks to cool.

Baking notes: For chocolate chocolate chip cookies, use a chocolate instant pudding in place of the vanilla pudding.

CHOCOLATE CHIP COOKIES II

Formed Cookies

YIELD: *3 to 5 dozen*
TOTAL TIME: *30 minutes*

½ cup butter, at room temperature
1 large egg, beaten
1 teaspoon vanilla extract
2 cups Basic Drop Cookie Mix (see p. 58)
½ cup semisweet chocolate chips

1 Preheat the oven to 350 degrees. Lightly grease 2 baking sheets.

2 In a large bowl, beat the butter, egg, and vanilla extract together. Gradually blend in the cookie mix. Fold in the chocolate chips.

3 Pinch off walnut-sized pieces of dough and roll into balls. Place 2 inches apart on the prepared baking sheets.

4 Bake for 10 to 14 minutes, until firm to the touch. Cool on the pans for 1 minute before transferring to wire racks to cool completely.

Baking notes: This dough can be used to make drop cookies. Bake for 8 to 10 minutes.

CHOCOLATE CHIP COOKIES III

Drop Cookies

YIELD: *3 to 5 dozen*
TOTAL TIME: *30 minutes*
CHILLING TIME: *1 hour*

2 cups all-purpose flour
1 teaspoon baking soda
½ teaspoon salt
1 cup vegetable shortening
½ cup granulated sugar
¾ cup packed light brown sugar
1 large egg
2½ teaspoons white crème de menthe
1⅓ cups (8 ounces) semisweet chocolate chips

1 Combine the flour, baking soda, and salt.

2 In a large bowl, cream the vegetable shortening and the two sugars. Beat in the egg and crème de menthe. Gradually blend in the dry ingredients. Fold in the chocolate chips. Cover and refrigerate for 1 hour.

3 Preheat the oven to 350 degrees. Lightly grease 2 baking sheets.

4 Drop the dough by spoonfuls 1½ inches apart onto the prepared baking sheets.

5 Bake for 10 to 12 minutes, until lightly colored. Transfer to wire racks to cool.

CHOCOLATE CRINKLES

Formed Cookies

YIELD: *3 to 4 dozen*
TOTAL TIME: *30 minutes*

2 cups all-purpose flour
2 teaspoons baking powder
3 ounces semisweet chocolate, chopped
½ cup canola oil
1½ cups granulated sugar
2 large eggs
¼ cup milk
1 teaspoon vanilla extract
Powdered sugar for rolling

1 Preheat the oven to 350 degrees. Lightly grease 2 baking sheets.

2 Combine the flour and baking powder.

3 Melt the chocolate in a double boiler over low heat, stirring until smooth. Remove from the heat.

4 In a large bowl, beat the canola oil and sugar until well blended. Beat in the eggs one at a time, beating well after each addition. Beat in the chocolate. Beat in the milk and vanilla extract. Gradually blend in the dry ingredients.

5 Pinch off walnut-sized pieces of dough and roll into balls. Roll in powdered sugar and place 1½ inches apart on the prepared baking sheets.

6 Bake for 12 to 15 minutes, or until firm to the touch. Roll in powdered sugar while still warm and transfer to wire racks to cool.

CHOCOLATE-FILLED PINWHEELS

Refrigerator Cookies
YIELD: *4 to 5 dozen*
TOTAL TIME: *45 minutes*
CHILLING TIME: *2 hours and overnight*

2 cups all-purpose flour
1 teaspoon baking powder
½ teaspoon salt
¾ cup vegetable shortening
1 cup granulated sugar
1 large egg
1 tablespoon vanilla extract

FILLING

1 cup (6 ounces) semisweet chocolate chips
2 tablespoons butter
1 cup walnuts, ground fine
½ tablespoon vanilla extract

1 Combine the flour, baking
powder, and salt.

2 Cream the vegetable shortening and sugar in a large bowl.
Beat in the egg. Beat in the
vanilla extract. Gradually blend
in the dry ingredients. Measure
out ⅔ cup of the dough and set
aside. Cover the remaining
dough and chill for 2 hours.

3 To make the filling, melt the
chocolate and butter in the top of
a double boiler over low heat,
string until smooth. Remove
from the heat and stir in the walnuts and vanilla extract. Blend in
the reserved dough.

4 On a floured surface, roll out
the chilled dough to a 16 by 12-

inch rectangle. Spread the chocolate mixture over the dough to
within ¼ inch of the edges. Starting on a long side, roll the dough
up jelly-roll fashion. Pinch the
seam to seal. Cut in half to make
two 8-inch logs. Wrap in waxed
paper and chill overnight.

5 Preheat the oven to 350
degrees.

6 Slice the logs into ¼-inch-thick
slices and place 1½ inches apart
on ungreased baking sheets.

7 Bake for 10 to 12 minutes, until
lightly colored. Transfer to wire
racks to cool.

Baking notes: To decorate, drizzle melted white or dark chocolate over the top of the cooled
cookies.

Chocolate Rum Balls

Formed Cookies

Yield: *2 to 3 dozen*
Total time: *30 minutes*
Sitting time: *1 hour*

1½ cups crushed chocolate wafer
   cookies
½ cup powdered sugar
½ cup walnuts, ground fine
¼ cup light corn syrup
3 tablespoons rum
Powdered sugar for rolling

1 In a large bowl, combine the
crushed cookies, powdered
sugar, and walnuts.

2 In a small saucepan, heat the
light corn syrup and rum until
warm. Add the dry ingredients
and blend thoroughly.

3 Pinch off walnut-sized pieces
of dough and roll into balls. Roll
in powdered sugar and place on
wire racks.

4 Let sit for 1 hour.

5 Roll the balls in powdered
sugar a second time. Store in an
airtight container.

Chocolate Sandwiches

Rolled Cookies

Yield: *3 to 4 dozen*
Total time: *45 minutes*

1¼ cups all-purpose flour
1 cup walnuts, ground fine
½ teaspoon salt
⅔ cup vegetable shortening
1 cup granulated sugar
1 teaspoon vanilla extract
¾ cup semisweet chocolate chips

1 Preheat the oven to 400
degrees. Lightly grease 2 baking
sheets.

2 Combine the flour, walnuts,
and salt.

3 In a large bowl, cream the vegetable shortening and sugar. Beat
in the vanilla. Gradually blend in
the dry ingredients.

4 On a floured surface, roll out
the dough to a thickness of ⅛
inch. Using a 2-inch fluted round
cookie cutter, cut the dough into
rounds and place 1 inch apart on
the prepared baking sheets.

5 Bake for 8 to 10 minutes, until
firm to the touch. Transfer to wire
racks to cool.

6 Melt the chocolate in a double
boiler over low heat, stirring
until smooth. Spread a thin layer
of chocolate on the bottom half of
the cookies and top with the
remaining cookies to form sandwich cookies.

Baking notes: These cookies
tend to be dry. This can be reme-
died by using Chocolate Butter
Cream for the filling (see Pantry).

CHOCOLATE SPARKLES

Formed Cookies

YIELD: *5 to 6 dozen*
TOTAL TIME: *30 minutes*
CHILLING TIME: *2 hours*

2 ounces semisweet chocolate, chopped
2⅔ cups all-purpose flour
2 teaspoons cream of tartar
1 teaspoon baking soda
¼ teaspoon salt
1 cup vegetable shortening
1¼ cups granulated sugar
2 large eggs
½ teaspoon vanilla extract
Granulated sugar for rolling

1 Melt the chocolate in a double boiler over low heat, stirring until smooth. Remove from the heat.

2 Combine the flour, cream of tartar, baking soda, and salt.

3 In a large bowl, cream the vegetable shortening and sugar. Beat in the eggs. Beat in the melted chocolate and vanilla extract. Gradually blend in the dry ingredients. Cover and chill for 2 hours.

4 Preheat the oven to 400 degrees.

5 Pinch off walnut-sized pieces and roll into balls. Roll in granulated sugar and place 1½ inches apart on ungreased baking sheets.

6 Bake for 8 to 10 minutes, until firm to the touch. Transfer to wire racks to cool.

CHOCOLATE SPICE DROPS

Drop Cookies

YIELD: *6 to 7 dozen*
TOTAL TIME: *30 minutes*

2 ounces bittersweet chocolate, chopped
3 cups all-purpose flour
1 cup walnuts, ground fine
1 teaspoon baking soda
1 teaspoon ground cinnamon
1 teaspoon ground allspice
½ teaspoon ground cloves
½ cup butter, at room temperature
1½ cups granulated sugar
2 large eggs
⅔ cup sour cream
1 cup raisins

1 Preheat the oven to 350 degrees.

2 Melt the chocolate in a double boiler over low heat, stirring until smooth. Remove from the heat.

3 Combine the flour, walnuts, baking soda, and spices.

4 In a large bowl, cream the butter and sugar. Beat in the eggs one at a time, beating vigorously after each addition. Beat in the sour cream and melted chocolate. Gradually blend in the dry ingredients. Fold in the raisins.

5 Drop the dough by spoonfuls 1½ inches apart onto ungreased baking sheets.

6 Bake for 18 to 20 minutes, until firm. Transfer to wire racks to cool.

CHRISTMAS COOKIES

Formed Cookies

YIELD: *5 to 6 dozen*
TOTAL TIME: *30 minutes*
CHILLLING TIME: *8 hours*

2 cups all-purpose flour
1 teaspoon baking soda
¼ teaspoon salt
½ cup vegetable shortening
⅔ cup packed light brown sugar
1 large egg
¼ cup cider vinegar
1½ teaspoons rum
½ cup flaked coconut
½ cup candied citrus peel, chopped fine
½ cup red and green glacé cherries
1 large egg white, beaten
¼ cup slivered almonds for the topping

1 Combine the flour, baking soda, and salt.

2 In a large bowl, cream the vegetable shortening and sugar. Beat in the egg. Beat in the vinegar and rum. Gradually blend in the dry ingredients. Fold in the coconut, candied citrus peel, and glacé cherries. Cover and chill for 8 hours or overnight.

3 Preheat the oven to 350 degrees. Lightly grease 2 baking sheets.

4 Working with one quarter of the dough at a time, pinch off walnut-sized pieces of dough and roll into balls. Place 2 inches apart on the prepared baking sheets. Flatten each ball with the bottom of a glass dipped in flour, then brush the cookies with the beaten egg white and sprinkle with the slivered almonds.

5 Bake for 8 to 10 minutes, until lightly colored. Transfer to wire racks to cool.

CHRISTMAS COOKIES II

Rolled Cookies

YIELD: *3 to 5 dozen*
TOTAL TIME: *30 minutes*
CHILLING TIME: *2 hours*

1½ cups all-purpose flour
¼ teaspoon ground cinnamon
½ teaspoon grated orange zest
¼ teaspoon grated lemon zest
6 tablespoons butter, at room temperature
¼ cup granulated sugar
1 large egg
2 tablespoons canola oil
1½ teaspoons white port
Powdered sugar for sprinkling

1 Combine the flour, cinnamon, and orange and lemon zest.

2 In a large bowl, cream the butter and sugar. Beat in the egg. Beat in the oil and wine. Gradually blend in the dry ingredients. Cover and chill 2 for hours.

3 Preheat the oven to 350 degrees. Lightly grease 2 baking sheets.

4 On a floured surface, roll out the dough to a thickness of ¼ inch. Using cookie cutters, cut into shapes and place 1½ inches apart on the prepared baking sheets.

5 Bake for 12 to 15 minutes, until lightly colored. Transfer to wire racks to cool.

6 When cool, sprinkle the cookies with powdered sugar.

CHRISTMAS COOKIES III

Rolled Cookies

YIELD: *4 to 5 dozen*
TOTAL TIME: *40 minutes*

2½ cups all-purpose flour
2 teaspoons baking powder
1 teaspoon ground cinnamon
1 cup butter, at room temperature
1 cup granulated sugar
2 large eggs
1 teaspoon almond extract
½ cup almonds, chopped
1 large egg white, beaten

1 Preheat the oven to 375 degrees. Lightly grease 2 baking sheets.

2 Combine the flour, baking powder, almonds, and cinnamon.

3 In a large bowl, cream the butter and sugar. Beat in the eggs. Beat in the almond extract. Gradually blend in the dry ingredients. Fold in the almonds.

4 On a floured surface, roll out the dough to a thickness of ¼ inch. Using cookie cutter, cut into shapes. Place 1½ inches apart on the prepared baking sheets and brush with the beaten egg white.

5 Bake for 10 to 12 minutes, until lightly colored. Transfer to wire racks to cool.

CHRISTMAS WREATHS

Formed Cookies

YIELD: *3 to 4 dozen*
TOTAL TIME: *30 minutes*

1 cup vegetable shortening
½ cup granulated sugar
1 large egg
1 teaspoon vanilla extract
2½ tablespoons all-purpose flour
1⅓ cups almonds, ground fine
¼ cup maple syrup
Red and green glacé cherries, halved

1 Preheat the oven to 350 degrees. Lightly grease 2 baking sheets.

2 In a large bowl, cream the vegetable shortening and sugar. Beat in the egg and vanilla extract. Gradually blend in the flour. Transfer one-third of the dough to a medium ball.

3 Fill a cookie press or a pastry bag fitted with a small star tip with the remaining dough and press or pipe out small rings onto the prepared baking sheets, spacing them 1 inch apart.

4 Add the almonds and maple syrup to the reserved cookie dough and blend well. Place ¼ to ½ teaspoon of this filling in the center of each ring, and place a half cherry at the point where the ends of each ring join.

5 Bake for 10 to 12 minutes, until lightly colored. Transfer to wire racks to cool.

Cinnamon Crisps

Formed Cookies

YIELD: *3 to 4 dozen*
TOTAL TIME: *30 minutes*

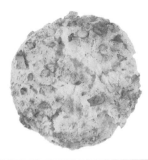

1¼ cups all-purpose flour
1 teaspoon baking soda
¼ teaspoon salt
½ cup vegetable shortening
1 cup granulated sugar
1 large egg
1 teaspoon almond extract
½ cup almonds, chopped fine
2 teaspoons ground cinnamon

1 Preheat the oven to 375 degrees. Lightly grease 2 baking sheets.

2 Combine the flour, baking soda, and salt.

3 In a large bowl, cream the vegetable shortening and sugar. Beat in the egg. Beat in the almond extract. Gradually blend in the dry ingredients.

4 Combine the almonds and cinnamon in a shallow dish.

5 Pinch off walnut-sized pieces of dough and roll into balls. Roll in the almond mixture and place 1½ inches apart on the prepared baking sheets.

6 Bake for 10 to 12 minutes, until lightly colored. Transfer to wire racks to cool.

Cocoa Drop Cookies

Drop Cookies

YIELD: *4 to 5 dozen*
TOTAL TIME: *40 minutes*

2 cups all-purpose flour
2 teaspoons baking powder
¼ teaspoon salt
6 tablespoons butter, at room temperature
1 cup granulated sugar
3 tablespoons unsweetened cocoa powder
3 large eggs
1 tablespoon milk
2 teaspoons vanilla extract
Walnut halves for decoration

1 Preheat the oven to 375 degrees. Lightly grease 2 baking sheets.

2 Combine the flour, baking powder, and salt.

3 In a large bowl, cream the butter and sugar. Beat in the cocoa. Beat in the eggs, milk, and vanilla extract.

4 Drop the dough by spoonfuls 1½ inches apart onto the prepared baking sheets. Press a walnut half into the center of each cookie.

5 Bake for 10 to 12 minutes, until firm to the touch. Transfer to wire racks to cool.

Coconut Butterballs

Formed Cookies

Yield: *3 to 4 dozen*
Total time: *30 minutes*
Chilling time: *4 hours*

2 cups all-purpose flour
½ teaspoon salt
1 cup butter, at room temperature
½ cup powdered sugar
2 teaspoons vanilla extract
1 cup flaked coconut
Powdered sugar for rolling

1 Combine the flour and salt.

2 In a large bowl, cream the butter and powdered sugar. Beat in the vanilla extract. Gradually blend in the dry ingredients. Fold in the coconut. Cover and chill for 4 hours.

3 Preheat the oven to 350 degrees.

4 Pinch off walnut-sized pieces of dough and roll into balls. Place each ball 1 inch apart on ungreased baking sheets.

5 Bake for 10 to 12 minutes, until lightly colored. Transfer to wire racks to cool.

6 Just before serving, roll the balls in powdered sugar.

Coconut Kisses

Drop Cookies

Yield: *2 to 3 dozen*
Total time: *55 minutes*

4 large egg whites
¼ teaspoon cream of tartar
¼ teaspoon salt
1 cup granulated sugar
¼ teaspoon almond extract
1½ cups flaked coconut

1 Preheat the oven to 250 degrees. Line 2 baking sheets with parchment paper.

2 In a large bowl, beat the egg whites until foamy. Beat in the cream of tartar and salt. Beat in the sugar a tablespoon at a time. Beat in the almond extract and beat until the whites hold stiff peaks. Gently fold in the coconut.

3 Drop the mixture by spoonfuls 1½ inches apart onto the prepared baking sheets.

4 Bake for 35 to 45 minutes, until firm to the touch. Transfer to wire racks to cool.

Baking notes: For crisper kisses, when the cookies are done, turn the oven off and let the cookies cool completely in the oven.

Coconut Macaroons I

Drop Cookies
Yield: *2 to 3 dozen*
Total time: *40 minutes*

½ cup shredded coconut
2 teaspoons cornstarch
⅛ teaspoon salt
3 large egg whites
1 cup granulated sugar
1 teaspoon vanilla extract

1 Preheat the oven to 275 degrees. Line 2 baking sheets with parchment paper.

2 Combine the coconut, cornstarch, and salt in a medium bowl and toss to mix.

3 In a large bowl, beat the egg whites until stiff but not dry. Fold in the sugar and vanilla extract. Gradually fold in the coconut mixture.

4 Drop the dough by spoonfuls 1½ inches apart onto the prepared baking sheets.

5 Bake for 28 to 30 minutes, until lightly colored. Transfer to wire racks to cool.

Coconut Macaroons II

Drop Cookies
Yield: *2 to 3 dozen*
Total time: *45 minutes*

1 large egg white
⅓ cup sweetened condensed milk
1 teaspoon vanilla extract
1½ cups shredded coconut

1 Preheat the oven to 300 degrees. Line 2 baking sheets with parchment paper.

2 In a large bowl, beat the egg white until stiff but not dry. Gently blend in the condensed milk and vanilla extract. Fold in the coconut.

3 Drop the mixture by teaspoonfuls 1½ inch apart onto the prepared baking sheets.

4 Bake for 20 to 30 minutes, until lightly colored. Let cool completely on the baking sheets.

COFFEE-FLAVORED MOLASSES COOKIES

Drop Cookies
YIELD: *3 to 5 dozen*
TOTAL TIME: *35 minutes*

4½ cups all-purpose flour
2 teaspoons ground ginger
2 teaspoons ground cinnamon
1 cup vegetable shortening
1 cup granulated sugar
1 large egg
1 tablespoon plus 1 teaspoon baking soda
¼ cup hot water
1 cup molasses, warmed
¾ cup strong brewed coffee

1 Preheat the oven to 375 degrees. Lightly grease 2 baking sheets.

2 Combine the flour, ginger, and cinnamon.

3 In a large bowl, cream the vegetable shortening and sugar. Beat in the egg.

4 Dissolve the baking soda in the hot water and add to the egg mixture, beating until smooth. Beat in the molasses and coffee. Gradually blend in the dry ingredients.

5 Drop the dough by spoonfuls 1½ inches apart onto the prepared baking sheets.

6 Bake for 8 to 10 minutes, until just starting to color. Transfer to a wire rack to cool.

COFFEE KISSES

Drop Cookies
YIELD: *2 to 3 dozen*
TOTAL TIME: *60 minutes*

1 tablespoon plus 1 teaspoon instant coffee powder
1 tablespoon boiling water
4 large egg whites
¼ teaspoon cream of tartar
¼ teaspoon salt
1 cups granulated sugar
1 teaspoon crème de cacao

1 Preheat the oven to 250 degrees. Line 2 baking sheets with parchment paper.

2 In a cup, dissolve the coffee powder in the boiling water. Let cool.

3 In a large bowl, beat the egg whites until foamy. Beat in the cream of tartar and salt. Beat in the sugar 1 tablespoon at a time. Beat in the crème de cacao and beat until the whites form stiff peaks. Fold in the coffee.

4 Drop the dough by spoonfuls 1 inch apart onto the prepared baking sheets.

5 Bake for 35 to 40 minutes, until firm to the touch. Cool completely on the baking sheets on wire racks.

Coffee Meringues

Drop Cookies

YIELD: *3 to 4 dozen*
TOTAL TIME: *30 minutes*

2 large egg whites
1 teaspoon salt
1⅓ cups granulated sugar
⅓ cup hazelnuts, chopped
2 teaspoons brewed coffee
½ teaspoon vanilla extract
1 tablespoon finely ground
    hazelnuts

1 Preheat the oven to 400
degrees. Line 2 baking sheets
with parchment paper.

2 In a large bowl, beat the egg
whites until foamy. Beat in the
salt. Gradually beat in the sugar
and beat until the whites form
stiff peaks. Fold in the chopped
hazelnuts. Fold in the coffee and
vanilla extract.

3 Drop the dough by spoonfuls
1½ inches apart onto the prepared baking sheets. Sprinkle
with the ground hazelnuts.

4 Bake for 8 to 10 minutes, until
firm to the touch. Transfer the
pans to wire racks to cool.

Coffee-Pumpkin Cookies

Drop Cookies

YIELD: *5 to 6 dozen*
TOTAL TIME: *30 minutes*

3½ cups all-purpose flour
1 teaspoon baking soda
2 teaspoons pumpkin pie spice
½ teaspoon salt
½ cup vegetable shortening
2 cups packed light brown sugar
2 large eggs
1¾ cups solid-pack pumpkin
½ cup brewed coffee
½ cup raisins
½ cup hazelnuts, chopped

1 Preheat the oven to 400
degrees.

2 Combine the flour, baking
soda, pumpkin pie spice, and
salt.

3 In a large bowl, cream the vegetable shortening and brown
sugar. Beat in the eggs one at a
time. Beat in the pumpkin and
coffee. Gradually blend in the
dry ingredients. Fold in the
raisins and hazelnuts.

4 Drop the dough by spoonfuls
1½ inches apart onto ungreased
baking sheets.

5 Bake for 10 to 12 minutes, until
golden brown. Transfer to wire
racks to cool.

COOKIE PIZZA

Formed Cookies

YIELD: *4 dozen*
TOTAL TIME: *30 minutes*

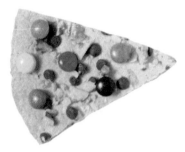

CRUST
¾ cup all-purpose flour
½ teaspoon baking powder
½ teaspoon baking soda
Pinch of salt
½ cup vegetable shortening
¾ cup packed light brown sugar
1 large egg
1 teaspoon vanilla extract
1 cup rolled oats
½ cup flaked coconut

TOPPING
1 cup (6 ounces) semisweet chocolate chips
1 cup walnuts, chopped
½ cup M&Ms

1 Preheat the oven to 350 degrees. Lightly grease a 14 to 15-inch pizza pan.

2 Combine the flour, baking powder, baking soda, and salt.

3 In a large bowl, cream the vegetable shortening and brown sugar. Beat in the egg and vanilla. Gradually blend in the dry ingredients. Fold in the oats and coconut.

4 Press the dough evenly into the prepared pan. Sprinkle the chocolate chips and walnuts evenly over the top.

5 Bake for 12 to 15 minutes, until lightly colored. Sprinkle the M&Ms over the hot cookies. Cool in the pan on a wire rack for a few minutes before cutting into wedges.

CRANBERRY COOKIES

Refrigerator Cookies

YIELD: *3 to 4 dozen*
TOTAL TIME: *45 minutes*
CHILLING TIME: *8 hours*

1½ cups all-purpose flour
½ teaspoon baking powder
¼ teaspoon salt
½ cup vegetable shortening
¾ cup powdered sugar
3 tablespoons milk
1 teaspoon Amaretto
¾ cup cranberries, fresh or dried, chopped fine (see Baking notes)
½ cup flaked coconut

1 Combine the flour, baking powder, and salt.

2 In a large bowl, cream the vegetable shortening and powdered sugar. Beat in the milk and Amaretto. Gradually blend in the dry ingredients. Fold in the cranberries.

3 Divide the dough in half. Form each half into a log 1½ inches in diameter. Roll in coconut. Wrap in waxed paper and chill for 8 hours.

4 Preheat the oven to 375 degrees.

5 Cut the logs into ¼-inch-thick slices and place each slice 1 inch apart on ungreased baking sheets.

6 Bake for 12 to 15 minutes, until lightly colored. Transfer to wire racks to cool.

Baking notes: If using dried cranberries, cover cranberries with boiling water and plump for 10 minutes before chopping.

CREAM CHEESE REFRIGERATOR COOKIES

Refrigerator Cookies

YIELD: *2 to 3 dozen*
TOTAL TIME: *30 minutes.*
CHILLING TIME: *4 hours*

1 cup all-purpose flour
3 tablespoons poppy seeds
¼ teaspoon salt
4 ounces cream cheese, at room temperature
⅓ cup canola oil
¼ cup honey, warmed

1 Combine the flour, poppy seeds, and salt.

2 In a large bowl, beat the cream cheese, oil, and honey until well blended and smooth. Gradually blend in the dry ingredients. Shape the dough into a log 2½ inches in diameter. Wrap in waxed paper and chill for 4 hours.

3 Preheat the oven to 400 degrees. Lightly grease 2 baking sheets.

4 Cut the log into ¼-inch-thick slices and place 1 inch apart on the prepared baking sheets.

5 Bake for 6 to 8 minutes, or until lightly browned. Transfer to wire racks to cool.

CREAM CHEESE TASTIES

Rolled Cookies

YIELD: *3½ dozen*
TOTAL TIME: *40 minutes*
CHILLING TIME: *8 hours*

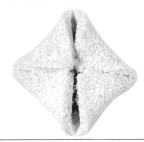

2 cups all-purpose flour
¼ teaspoon salt
1 cup vegetable shortening
8 ounces cream cheese, at room temperature
½ cup powdered sugar
About ¼ cup raspberry preserves
Powdered sugar for sprinkling

1 Combine the flour and salt.

2 In a large bowl, beat the vegetable shortening, cream cheese, and powdered sugar until smooth. Gradually blend in the dry ingredients. Divide the dough in half. Wrap each half in waxed paper and chill for 8 hours.

3 Preheat the oven to 375 degrees.

4 On a floured surface, roll out one-half of the dough to a rectangle approximately 10 inches by 11½ inches. Trim the edges of the dough and cut lengthwise into 4 strips. Cut each strip into 5 squares. Place ¼ teaspoon raspberry preserves in the center of each square and fold the dough over to form a triangle. Press the edges together to seal and place 1 inch apart on ungreased baking sheets. Repeat with the other half of the dough.

5 Bake for 10 to 12 minutes, until lightly colored. Sprinkle with powdered sugar and transfer to wire racks to cool.

Baking notes: Use fluted pastry cutter to cut the dough into decorative shapes if you like.

Cut-Out Hanukkah Cookies

Rolled Cookies

YIELD: *3 to 4 dozen*
TOTAL TIME: *30 minutes*
CHILLING TIME: *6 hours*

2½ cups all-purpose flour
1¼ teaspoons baking powder
⅛ teaspoon salt
¼ cup canola oil
¾ cup powdered sugar
1 large egg
¼ cup milk
1 teaspoon vanilla extract
1 teaspoon grated lemon zest
Vanilla Icing (see Pantry)

1 Combine the flour, baking powder, and salt.

2 In a large bowl, beat the oil and sugar. Beat in the egg. Beat in the milk and vanilla extract. Beat in the lemon zest. Gradually blend in the dry ingredients. Cover and chill for 6 hours.

3 Preheat the oven to 350 degrees.

4 On a floured surface, roll out the dough to a thickness of ⅛ inch. Using cookie cutters, cut into shapes and place 1½ inches apart on ungreased baking sheets.

5 Bake for 6 to 8 minutes, until lightly colored. Transfer to wire racks to cool before decorating with the icing.

Date Balls

Formed Cookies

YIELD: *4 to 5 dozen*
TOTAL TIME: *30 minutes*

1¼ cups all-purpose flour
Pinch of salt
½ cup vegetable shortening
⅓ cup powdered sugar
1 tablespoon water
1 teaspoon vanilla extract
⅔ cup dates, pitted and chopped
½ cup walnuts, chopped
Powdered sugar for rolling

1 Preheat the oven to 300 degrees.

2 Combine the flour and salt.

3 In a large bowl, cream the vegetable shortening and powdered sugar. Beat in the water and vanilla extract. Gradually blend in the dry ingredients. Fold in the dates and walnuts.

4 Pinch off 1-inch pieces of dough and roll into balls. Place 1 inch apart on the ungreased baking sheets.

5 Bake for 18 to 20 minutes, or just until the cookies start to color slightly. Roll in powdered sugar and transfer to wire racks to cool.

DATE-FILLED COOKIES

Rolled Cookies

YIELD: *2 to 3 dozen*
TOTAL TIME: *45 minutes*
CHILLING TIME: *4 hours*

3 cups all-purpose flour
½ teaspoon baking soda
¼ teaspoon salt
1 cup vegetable shortening
½ cup granulated sugar
½ cup packed light brown sugar
1 large egg
1 teaspoon vanilla extract

FILLING
2 cups dates, pitted and chopped
⅓ cup granulated sugar
½ cup water
2 tablespoons fresh lemon juice
¼ teaspoon salt
1 large egg, beaten
Granulated sugar for sprinkling

1 Combine the flour, baking soda, and salt.

2 In a large bowl, cream the vegetable shortening and two sugars. Beat in the egg. Beat in the vanilla extract. Gradually blend in the dry ingredients. Divide the dough in half. Wrap each half in waxed paper and chill for 4 hours.

3 To make the filling, combine the dates, sugar, water, lemon juice, and salt in a saucepan and cook, stirring until very thick. Remove from the heat.

4 Preheat the oven to 350 degrees.

5 On a floured surface, roll out the dough to a thickness of ⅛ inch. Using a 2½-inch round cookie cutter, cut out an equal number of cookies. Place half the rounds 1½ inches apart on ungreased baking sheets. Brush lightly with water and place a level tablespoonful of filling in the center of each round. Place the remaining rounds on top, and crimp the edges with a fork to seal. Make 2 slits in the top of each round and brush the tops with the beaten egg. Sprinkle with granulated sugar.

6 Bake for 10 to 12 minutes, until lightly colored. Transfer to wire racks to cool

DATE DROPS

Drop Cookies

YIELD: *1 to 2 dozen*
TOTAL TIME: *40 minutes*

1¼ cups all-purpose flour
½ teaspoon baking powder
½ teaspoon baking soda
¼ teaspoon salt
¼ cup vegetable shortening
¾ cup packed light brown sugar
1 large egg
½ cup sour cream
1 pound dates, pitted and chopped
About ½ cup walnuts
Vanilla Icing (see Pantry)

1 Preheat the oven to 400 degrees. Lightly grease 2 baking sheets.

2 Combine the flour, baking powder, baking soda, and salt.

3 In a large bowl, cream the vegetable shortening and brown sugar. Beat in the egg and sour cream. Gradually blend in the dry ingredients. Fold in the dates.

4 Drop the dough by spoonfuls 1½ inches apart onto the prepared baking sheets. Press a walnut into the center of each cookie.

5 Bake for 8 to 10 minutes, until lightly colored. Transfer to wire racks to cool.

6 Fill a pastry bag fitted with a small plain tip with the icing and pipe a ring of icing around each walnut.

Baking notes: In an old version of this recipe, whole pitted dates are stuffed with walnut halves and placed on baking sheets, then the dough is dropped on top of the dates.

DROP COOKIES

Drop Cookies

YIELD: *3 to 4 dozen*
TOTAL TIME: *30 minutes*

3 cups all-purpose flour
1 tablespoon baking powder
¼ teaspoon salt
⅔ cup butter, at room temperature
1½ cups granulated sugar
2 large eggs
¼ cup fresh orange juice
1 tablespoon water
½ teaspoon almond extract
1 tablespoon grated orange zest
1 cup raisins, chopped

1 Preheat the oven to 375 degrees. Lightly grease 2 baking sheets.

2 Combine the flour, baking powder, and salt.

3 In a large bowl, cream the butter and sugar. Beat in the eggs one at a time. Beat in orange juice, water, and almond extract. Beat in the orange zest. Gradually blend in the dry ingredients. Fold in the raisins.

4 Drop the dough by spoonfuls 1½ inches apart onto the prepared baking sheets.

5 Bake for 10 to 12 minutes, until lightly colored. Transfer to wire racks to cool.

Easy Fudge Cookies

Refrigerator Cookies

YIELD: *6 to 7 dozen*
TOTAL TIME: *35 minutes*
CHILLING TIME: *8 hours*

2 ounces semisweet chocolate, chopped
4⅓ cups all-purpose flour
1 teaspoon baking powder
½ teaspoon baking soda
¼ teaspoon salt
1 cup vegetable shortening
1 cup packed light brown sugar
1 cup granulated sugar
2 large eggs
⅓ cup milk
1 teaspoon vanilla extract
½ cup walnuts, chopped (optional)

1 Melt the chocolate in a double boiler over low heat, stirring until smooth. Remove from the heat.

2 Combine the flour, baking powder, baking soda, and salt.

3 In a large bowl, cream the vegetable shortening and two sugars. Beat in the eggs one at a time. Beat in the milk and vanilla extract. Beat in the melted chocolate. Gradually blend in the dry ingredients. Fold in the walnuts.

4 Divide the dough in half. Form each half into a 2-inch-thick logs. Wrap in waxed paper and chill for 8 hours or overnight.

5 Preheat the oven to 375 degrees.

6 Cut the logs into ⅛-inch-thick slices and place 1 inch apart on ungreased baking sheets.

7 Bake for 12 to 15 minutes, until lightly colored. Transfer to wire racks to cool.

English Tea Cakes

Formed Cookies

YIELD: *3 to 4 dozen*
TOTAL TIME: *50 minutes*
CHILLING TIME: *4 hours*

1¾ cups all-purpose flour
1½ teaspoons baking powder
¼ teaspoon salt
½ cup butter, at room temperature
¾ cup granulated sugar
1 large egg
2 tablespoons milk
½ cup candied citron, chopped fine
½ cup currants
1 large egg white
Granulated sugar for coating

1 Combine the flour, baking powder and salt.

2 In a large bowl, cream the butter and sugar. Beat in the egg and milk. Gradually blend in the dry ingredients. Fold in the candied citron and currants. Cover and chill for 4 hours.

3 Preheat the oven to 400 degrees. Lightly grease 2 baking sheets.

4 In a small bowl, beat the egg white until foamy.

5 Pinch off walnut-sized pieces of dough and roll into balls. Dip half of each ball in the beaten egg white and then in granulated sugar and place the balls, sugar side up, 1½ inches apart on the prepared baking sheets.

6 Bake for 12 to 15 minutes, until lightly colored. Transfer to wire racks to cool.

FINNISH COOKIES

Rolled Cookies

YIELD: *4 to 5 dozen*
TOTAL TIME: *35 mintues*

2¼ cup all-purpose flour
2 teaspoons unsweetened cocoa
  powder
¾ cup vegetable shortening
1 cup powdered sugar
¾ cup vanilla extract

1 Preheat the oven to 350
degrees. Lightly grease 2 baking
sheets.

2 Combine the flour and cocoa
powder.

3 In a large bowl, cream the vegetable shortening and powdered
sugar. Beat in the vanilla extract.
Gradually blend in the dry
ingredients.

4 On a floured surface, roll out
the dough to a thickness of ¼
inch. Using cookie cutters, cut
out cookies and place them 1
inch apart on the prepared baking sheets.

5 Bake for 12 to 15 minutes, until
lightly colored. Transfer to wire
racks to cool.

FROSTED CHOCOLATE DROPS

Drop Cookies

YIELD: *3 to 4 dozen*
TOTAL TIME: *30 minutes*

1¾ cups all-purpose flour
½ teaspoon baking soda
½ teaspoon salt
2 ounces unsweetened chocolate,
  chopped
½ cup vegetable shortening
¾ cups granulated sugar
1 large egg
½ cup evaporated milk
1 teaspoon vanilla extract
½ cup walnuts, chopped
Chocolate Icing (see Pantry)

1 Preheat the oven to 375
degrees. Lightly grease 2 baking
sheets.

2 Combine the flour, baking
soda, and salt.

3 In the top of a double boiler,
melt the chocolate and vegetable
shortening, stirring until smooth.
Remove from the heat and beat
in the sugar. Beat in the egg. Beat
in the milk and vanilla extract.
Gradually blend in the dry ingredients. Fold in the chopped
walnuts.

4 Drop the dough by spoonfuls
1½ inches apart onto the prepared baking sheets.

5 Bake for 12 to 15 minutes, until
firm to the touch. Transfer to wire
racks to cool.

6 Frost the cookies with the
chocolate icing.

FLORENTINES

Drop Cookies

YIELD: *2 to 4 dozen*
TOTAL TIME: *30 minutes*

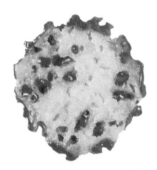

¾ cup almonds, ground fine
¼ cup all-purpose flour
¼ cup butter
⅓ cup granulated sugar
5 tablespoons heavy cream
½ cup grated orange zest

TOPPING
4 ounces semisweet chocolate, chopped
3 tablespoons butter

1 Preheat the oven to 375 degrees. Lightly grease and flour 2 baking sheets.

2 Combine the almonds and flour.

3 Combine the butter, sugar, and cream in a saucepan and bring to a boil. Remove from the heat and gradually blend in the dry ingredients. Stir in the orange zest. The mixture will be very thin.

4 Drop the batter by tablespoonfuls 3 inches apart onto the prepared baking sheets. With the back of a spoon dipped in flour, spread the batter into 2-inch rounds.

5 Bake for 12 to 15 minutes, until the edges start to brown (the cen-ters may still look bubbly). Cool on the baking sheets on wire racks.

6 For the topping, melt the chocolate and butter in the top of a double boiler, stirring until smooth. Remove from the heat.

7 Place the cooled cookies upside down on the wire racks. Using a pastry brush, paint a thin layer of the melted chocolate over the bottom of each one. Let cool until the chocolate sets.

FRUIT COOKIES

Drop Cookies
YIELD: *5 to 6 dozen*
TOTAL TIME: *30 minutes*

2 cups all-purpose flour
1 teaspoon baking powder
½ teaspoon baking soda
2 teaspoons ground allspice
¼ teaspoon salt
1 cup granulated sugar
⅓ cup vegetable oil
2 large eggs
2 cups raisins
⅓ cup almonds, chopped

1 Preheat the oven to 375 degrees. Lightly grease 2 baking sheets.

2 Combine the flour, baking powder, baking soda, allspice, and salt.

3 In a large bowl, beat the sugar and vegetable oil. Beat in the eggs. Gradually blend in the dry ingredients. Stir in the raisins and almonds.

4 Drop the dough by spoonfuls 1½ inches apart onto the prepared baking sheets.

5 Bake for 10 to 12 minutes, until lightly colored and firm to the touch. Transfer to wire racks to cool.

FRUIT DROPS

Drop Cookies
YIELD: *2 to 3 dozen*
TOTAL TIME: *30 minutes*

1 cup cornflakes, crushed
2 cups shredded coconut
½ teaspoon salt
1 cup sweetened condensed milk
1 cup dates, pitted and chopped fine
1 cup pitted prunes, chopped fine
1 cup figs, chopped fine
1 cup golden raisins, chopped fine
1 cup currants

1 Preheat the oven to 350 degrees. Lightly grease 2 baking sheets.

2 In a large bowl, combine the cornflakes, coconut, and salt. Stir in the condensed milk. Stir in all the fruit and blend thoroughly.

3 Drop the mixture by spoonfuls 1 inch apart onto the prepared baking sheets.

4 Bake for 12 to 15 minutes, until golden colored. Transfer to wire racks to cool.

Baking notes: If you like, drizzle melted chocolate or vanilla icing over the top of the cooled cookies.

FUDGIES I

Drop Cookies
YIELD: *4 to 6 dozen*
TOTAL TIME: *30 minutes*

2 cups all-purpose flour
½ cup unsweetened cocoa powder
½ teaspoon baking soda
¼ teaspoon salt
¼ cup vegetable shortening
½ cup granulated sugar
1 large egg
½ cup buttermilk
½ cup molasses
1 teaspoon vanilla extract
¾ cup walnuts, chopped

1 Preheat the oven to 350 degrees. Lightly grease 2 baking sheets.

2 Combine the flour, cocoa powder, baking soda, and salt.

3 In a large bowl, cream the vegetable shortening and sugar. Beat in the egg. Beat in the buttermilk and molasses. Beat in the vanilla extract. Gradually blend in the dry ingredients. Fold in the walnuts.

4 Drop the dough by spoonfuls 1½ inches apart onto the prepared baking sheets.

5 Bake for 12 to 15 minutes, until firm to the touch. Transfer to wire racks to cool.

Baking notes: Sour milk can be used in place of the buttermilk.

GERMAN ALMOND WAFERS

Formed Cookies
YIELD: *2 to 3 dozen*
TOTAL TIME: *30 minutes*

1⅔ cups all-purpose flour
2 teaspoons baking powder
½ cup vegetable shortening
1 cup granulated sugar
1 large egg
1 teaspoon vanilla extract

TOPPING
⅔ cup heavy cream
2 teaspoons granulated sugar
1 cup sliced almonds

1 Combine the flour and baking powder.

2 In a large bowl, cream the vegetable shortening and sugar. Beat in the egg. Beat in the vanilla extract. Gradually blend in the dry ingredients. Cover and chill for 4 hours.

3 To prepare the topping, combine the cream and sugar in a saucepan. Remove from the heat and add the almonds.

4 Preheat the oven to 350 degrees. Lightly grease 2 baking sheets.

5 Pinch off walnut-sized pieces of dough and roll into balls. Place 1½ inches apart on the prepared baking sheets. Using the bottom of a glass dipped in flour, flatten each ball to a thickness of ¼ inch. Spread a teaspoon of the topping over each cookie.

6 Bake for 10 to 14 minutes, until lightly colored. Transfer to wire racks to cool.

German Bonbons

Formed Cookies

YIELD: *4 to 6 dozen*
TOTAL TIME: *45 minutes*
CHILLING TIME: *1 hour*

3 large egg whites
2 cups powdered sugar
1 pound hazelnuts, toasted and ground
Powdered sugar for shaping
6 ounces semisweet chocolate

1 Preheat the oven to 350 degrees. Line 2 baking sheets with waxed paper.

2 Combine the eggs, sugar, and hazelnuts in a food processor or blender, and process to a paste.

3 Dust your hands with powdered sugar. Pinch off 1-inch pieces of dough and roll into balls. Place 1 inch apart on the prepared baking sheets.

4 Bake for 10 to 12 minutes, until firm to the touch. Transfer to wire racks to cool.

5 Melt the chocolate in the top of a double boiler over low heat, stirring until smooth. Remove from the heat and keep warm over hot water.

6 One at a time, insert a bamboo skewer into each ball and dip in the melted chocolate. Let the excess drip off and chill for at least 1 hour on wire racks

Baking notes: If the hazelnut dough seems too dry, add additional egg whites, one at a time. If it seems too wet, add more ground hazelnuts. Substitute almonds, brazil nuts, or even chestnuts for the hazelnuts.

German Spice Cookies

Rolled Cookies

YIELD: *2 to 4 dozen*
TOTAL TIME: *35 minutes*
CHILLING TIME: *8 hours*

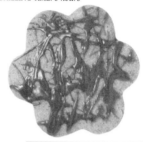

4 cups all-purpose flour
2 cups walnuts, ground
2 teaspoons baking powder
¼ teaspoon paprika
¼ teaspoon freshly ground black pepper
¼ teaspoon ground ginger
¼ teaspoon ground cloves
¼ teaspoon ground coriander
¼ teaspoon anise seeds
1½ cups vegetable shortening
1 cup granulated sugar
1 large egg

1 Combine the flour, walnuts, baking powder, and spices.

2 In a large bowl, cream the vegetable shortening with the sugar until light and fluffy. Beat in the egg. Gradually blend in the dry ingredients. Cover and chill for 8 hours.

3 Preheat the oven to 350 degrees.

4 On a floured surface, roll out the dough to a thickness of ¼ inch. Using a 2-inch round cookie cutter, cut into rounds and place 1½ inches apart on ungreased baking sheets.

5 Bake for 15 to 18 minutes, until lightly colored. Transfer to wire racks to cool.

Baking notes: If desired, drizzle melted chocolate over the cooled cookies.

Gingerbread Cookies

Rolled Cookies

Yield: *8 to 10 dozen*
Total time: *35 minutes*
Chilling time: *24 hours*

6½ cups all-purpose flour
1 teaspoon ground ginger
1 teaspoon ground cinnamon
¼ teaspoon ground cloves
2 teaspoons salt
1 cup vegetable shortening
1 cup packed light brown sugar
2 teaspoons baking soda
½ teaspoon warm water
1½ cups molasses

1 Combine the flour, spices, and salt.

2 In a large bowl, cream the vegetable shortening and brown sugar.

3 Dissolve the baking soda in the warm water and add to the creamed mixture, beating until smooth. Beat in the molasses. Gradually blend in the dry ingredients. Cover and chill for 24 hours.

4 Preheat the oven to 350 degrees. Lightly grease 2 baking sheets.

5 On a floured surface, roll out the dough to a thickness of ¼ inch. Using a 1¾-inch round cookie cutter, cut out cookies and place 1½ inches apart on the prepared baking sheets.

6 Bake for 10 to 12 minutes, until dry-looking and firm to the touch. Transfer to wire racks to cool.

Baking notes: This dough can be used for making gingerbread houses or gingerbread men (see Pantry); it can also be pressed into large cookie molds and baked.

Ginger Butter Treats

Rolled Cookies

Yield: *2 to 4 dozen*
Total time: *35 minutes*

4 cups all-purpose flour
1 tablespoon ground ginger
1 teaspoon ground cinnamon
½ teaspoon salt
1 cup butter, at room temperature
1¼ cups packed light brown sugar
2 large eggs
½ teaspoon grated lemon zest

1 Preheat the oven to 350 degrees. Lightly grease 2 baking sheets.

2 Combine the flour, ginger, cinnamon, and salt.

3 In a large bowl, cream the butter and brown sugar. Beat in the eggs. Beat in the lemon zest. Gradually blend in the dry ingredients.

4 On a flour surface, roll out the dough to a thickness of ¼ inch. Using a 2-inch round cookie cutter, cut out cookies and place 1 inch apart on the prepared baking sheets.

5 Bake for 12 to 15 minutes, until lightly colored. Transfer to wire racks to cool.

Ginger Crinkles

Formed Cookies

YIELD: *4 to 5 dozen*
TOTAL TIME: *40 minutes*

2 cups all-purpose flour
2 teaspoons baking soda
1 teaspoon ground cinnamon
1 teaspoon ground ginger
¼ teaspoon salt
1 cup granulated sugar
⅔ cup canola oil
1 large egg
¼ cup molasses, warmed
Granulated sugar for rolling

1 Preheat the oven to 350 degrees.

2 Combine the flour, baking soda, spices, and salt.

3 In a large bowl, beat the sugar and oil together. Beat in the egg. Beat in the molasses. Gradually blend in the dry ingredients.

4 Pinch off walnut-sized pieces of dough and roll into balls. Roll in granulated sugar until well coated and place the balls 3 inches apart on ungreased baking sheets.

5 Bake for 12 to 15 minutes, until lightly colored. Transfer to wire racks to cool.

Baking notes: The dough can also be dropped by spoonfuls into a bowl of sugar and then rolled into balls.

Gingersnaps I

Rolled Cookies

YIELD: *2 to 3 dozen*
TOTAL TIME: *30 minutes*
CHILLING TIME: *4 hours*

3 cups all-purpose flour
1 teaspoon baking powder
1 teaspoon ground ginger
1 teaspoon ground cinnamon
½ teaspoon salt
½ cup granulated sugar
¾ cup vegetable shortening
½ cup heavy cream
¼ cup light corn syrup

1 Combine the flour, baking powder, spices, and salt.

2 In a large bowl, cream the sugar and vegetable shortening. Beat in the cream and corn syrup. Gradually blend in the dry ingredients. Cover and chill for 4 hours.

3 Preheat the oven to 350 degrees. Lightly grease 2 baking sheets.

4 On a floured surface, roll out the dough to a thickness of ¼ inch. Using a 3-inch round cookie cutter, cut into rounds and place 1 inch apart on the prepared baking sheets.

5 Bake for 10 to 12 minutes, until lightly colored. Transfer to wire racks to cool.

Baking notes: If you like spicy gingersnaps, you can add up to 1 tablespoon ground ginger to the dough.

Gingersnaps II

Rolled Cookies

Yield: 3 to 4 dozen
Total time: 35 minutes
Chilling time: 4 hours

3 cups all-purpose flour
1 tablespoon ground ginger
1 teaspoon salt
¾ cup vegetable shortening
½ cup granulated sugar
1 cup molasses, warmed

1 Combine the flour, ginger, and salt.

2 In a large bowl, cream the vegetable shortening and sugar. Beat in the molasses. Gradually blend in the dry ingredients. Cover and chill for 4 hours.

3 Preheat the oven to 350 degrees. Lightly grease 2 baking sheets.

4 On a floured surface, roll out the dough to a thickness of ¼ inch. Using a 1¾-inch round cookie cutter, cut into rounds and place 1 inch apart on the prepared baking sheets.

5 Bake for 10 to 12 minutes, until lightly colored and firm to the touch. Transfer to wire racks to cool.

Granny's Cookies

Rolled Cookies

Yield: 7 to 8 dozen
Total time: 40 minutes

4 cups all-purpose flour
1 tablespoon baking powder
¼ teaspoon ground nutmeg
¾ cup vegetable shortening
2 cups granulated sugar
2 large eggs
¼ cup milk
1 teaspoon vanilla extract

1 Preheat the oven to 400 degrees. Lightly grease 2 baking sheets.

2 Combine the flour, baking powder, and nutmeg.

3 In a large bowl, cream the vegetable shortening and sugar. Beat in the eggs one at a time. Beat in the milk and vanilla extract. Gradually blend in the dry ingredients.

4 On a floured surface, roll out the dough to a thickness of ¼ inch. Using cookie cutters, cut into shapes and place 1½ inches apart into the prepared baking sheets.

5 Bake for 10 to 12 minutes, until lightly colored. Transfer to wire racks to cool.

Baking notes: To decorate these cookies, sprinkle with colored sugar crystals or place a raisin or walnut half in the center of each one before baking.

Granola Cookies

Drop Cookies

Yield: *3 to 5 dozen*
Total time: *30 minutes.*

2 cups all-purpose flour
½ teaspoon baking powder
1 teaspoon ground cinnamon
½ teaspoon ground nutmeg
2 cups granola
2 tablespoons canola oil
2 large eggs
1 cup unsweetened applesauce
2 tablespoons frozen apple juice
    concentrate, thawed

1 Preheat the oven to 350 degrees. Lightly grease 2 baking sheets.

2 Combine the flour, baking powder, and spices.

3 In a large bowl, beat the canola oil and eggs together. Beat in the applesauce and apple juice. Gradually blend in the dry ingredients. Stir in the granola.

4 Drop the mixture by spoonfuls 1½ inches apart onto the prepared baking sheets.

5 Bake for 8 to 10 minutes, until lightly colored and firm to the touch. Transfer to wire racks to cool.

Greek Sesame Cookies

Formed Cookies

Yield: *3 dozen*
Total time: *45 minutes*

2⅓ cups all-purpose flour
1 teaspoon baking powder
¼ teaspoon salt
½ cup vegetable shortening
½ cup granulated sugar
2 large egg yolks
3 tablespoons heavy cream
1 large egg yolk beaten with 1 table-
    spoon heavy cream
3 tablespoons sesame seeds

1 Preheat the oven to 350 degrees.

2 Combine the flour, baking powder, and salt.

3 In a large bowl, cream the vegetable shortening and sugar. Beat in the egg yolks. Beat in the cream. Gradually blend in the dry ingredients.

4 Pinch off walnut-sized pieces of the dough and form into 7-inch ropes. Fold each rope in half and twist to form a braid, leaving an open loop at the top. Place the twists 1 inch apart on ungreased baking sheets.

5 Brush the twists with the beaten egg yolk and sprinkle with the sesame seeds.

6 Bake for 12 to 14 minutes, until golden brown. Transfer to wire racks to cool.

Greek Shortbread

Rolled Cookies

YIELD: *3 to 4 dozen*
TOTAL TIME: *45 minutes*
CHILLING TIME: *4 hours*

3½ cups all-purpose flour
½ teaspoon baking powder
½ teaspoon baking soda
1 cup vegetable shortening
¾ cup granulated sugar
2 large egg yolks
¼ teaspoon brandy
⅛ teaspoon rose water
½ cup almonds, ground

1 Combine the flour, baking powder, and baking soda.

2 In a large bowl, cream the vegetable shortening and sugar. Beat in the egg yolks. Beat in the brandy and rose water. Gradually blend in the dry ingredients. Cover and chill for 4 hours.

3 Preheat the oven to 325 degrees.

4 On a floured surface, roll out the dough to a thickness of ¼ inch. Using a 1½-inch round cookie cutter, cut out cookies. Dredge in the ground almonds and place 1 inch apart on ungreased baking sheets.

5 Bake for 25 to 30 minutes, until lightly colored. Transfer to wire racks to cool.

Green Wreaths

Formed Cookies

YIELD: *2 to 3 dozen*
TOTAL TIME: *30 minutes*

6 tablespoons vegetable shortening
32 marshmallows
½ teaspoon vanilla extract
½ teaspoon almond extract
½ teaspoon green food coloring
4 cups cornflakes, crushed
Red cinnamon candy

1 Line 2 baking sheets with waxed paper.

2 In the top of a double boiler, melt the vegetable shortening with the marshmallows. Add the vanilla and almond extracts. Stir in the food coloring. Remove from the heat and stir in the cornflakes. Replace over bottom half of double boiler to keep warm.

3 Drop the mix by tablespoonful 2 inches apart onto the prepared baking sheets. With well-oiled hands, form the batter into wreath shapes. Decorate with cinnamon candy and chill until set.

Baking notes: These are great cookies to let kids play with. You mix them and let the children form them. To give a more festive taste, use a few drops of peppermint in place of the vanilla and almond extracts.

Hazelnut Crescents I

Formed Cookies

YIELD: *2 to 3 dozen*
TOTAL TIME: *40 minutes*

¾ cup butter, at room temperature
½ cup granulated sugar
½ teaspoon almond extract
½ teaspoon vanilla extract
2 cups all-purpose flour
½ cup hazelnuts, chopped fine
Powdered sugar for rolling

1 Preheat the oven to 300 degrees.

2 In a large bowl, cream the butter and sugar. Beat in the almond and vanilla extracts. Gradually blend in the flour. Fold in the hazelnuts. The dough will be stiff.

3 Pinch off walnut-sized pieces of dough and form each one into a crescent shape. Place 1½ inches apart on ungreased baking sheets.

4 Bake for 15 to 20 minutes, until lightly colored. Roll in powdered sugar and transfer to wire racks to cool.

Hazelnut Crescents II

Formed Cookies

YIELD: *2 to 3 dozen*
TOTAL TIME: *30 minutes*

1¼ cups all-purpose flour
½ teaspoon baking powder
¼ teaspoon salt
½ cup vegetable shortening
½ cup powdered sugar
⅓ cup hazelnuts, chopped

1 Preheat the oven to 350 degrees.

2 Combine the flour, baking powder, and salt.

3 In a large bowl, cream the vegetable shortening and powdered sugar. Gradually blend in the dry ingredients. Fold in the hazelnuts.

4 Pinch off walnut-sized pieces of the dough and form into crescent shapes. Place 1 inch apart on ungreased baking sheets.

5 Bake for 10 to 12 minutes, until lightly colored. Transfer to wire racks to cool.

Hazelnut Fruit Rings

Formed Cookies
Yield: *1 to 2 dozen*
Total time: *35 minutes*

1 cup vegetable shortening
¾ cup packed light brown sugar
3 large egg yolks
1 teaspoon rum
2½ cups all-purpose flour
¾ cup hazelnuts, chopped
½ cup mixed candied fruit, chopped fine
1 large egg white
1 tablespoon light corn syrup
Glacè cherries, halved, for decoration

1 Preheat the oven to 325 degrees. Lightly grease 2 baking sheets.

2 In a large bowl, cream the vegetable shortening and brown sugar. Beat in the egg yolks. Beat in the rum. Gradually blend in the flour. Fold in the hazelnuts and candied fruit.

3 In a small cup, beat the egg white and corn syrup together.

4 Pinch off pieces of dough and roll into pencil-thin ropes about 6 inches long. Form the ropes into circles, pinch the ends together to seal, and place 1 inch apart on the prepared baking sheets. Place a half-cherry on each rope at the point where the ends meet. Brush the cookies with the corn syrup mixture.

5 Bake for 18 to 20 minutes, until lightly colored. Transfer to wire racks to cool.

Baking notes: Sprinkle the cookies with colored sugar crystals before baking if desired.

Hazelnut Shortbread

Formed Cookies
Yield: *4 to 5 dozen*
Total time: *30 minutes*

4½ cups all-purpose flour
1 cup hazelnuts, ground
2 cups vegetable shortening
2½ cups packed light brown sugar
2 teaspoons sherry

1 Preheat the oven to 350 degrees.

2 Combine the flour and hazelnuts.

3 In a large bowl, cream the vegetable shortening and brown sugar. Beat in the sherry. Gradually blend in the dry ingredients.

4 Pinch off walnut-sized pieces of dough and roll into small balls. Place 2 inches apart on ungreased bakings sheets. Flatten the balls with the bottom of a glass dipped in flour.

5 Bake for 12 to 15 minutes, until lightly colored. Transfer to wire racks to cool.

Holiday Wreaths

Formed Cookies
YIELD: *3 to 4 dozen*
TOTAL TIME: *30 minutes*

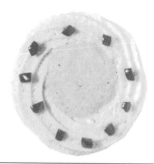

1 cup vegetable shortening
½ cup granulated sugar
1 large egg
1 teaspoon vanilla extract
2½ tablespoons all-purpose flour
¼ cup maple syrup
1⅓ cup walnuts, chopped
Red and green glacé cherries,
  chopped, for decoration

1 Preheat the oven to 350 degrees. Lightly grease 2 baking sheets.

2 In a large bowl, cream the vegetable shortening and sugar. Beat in the egg. Beat in the vanilla extract. Gradually blend in the flour. Transfer one-third of the dough to a medium bowl.

3 Place the remaining dough in a cookie press or pastry bag fitted with a small plain tip, and press or pipe out rings onto the prepared baking sheets, spacing them 2 inches apart.

4 Stir the maple syrup into the reserved dough. Stir in the walnuts. Fill the centers of the rings with the maple syrup mix.

5 Bake for 12 to 15 minutes, until lightly colored. Transfer to wire racks and decorate with the glacé cherries. Let cool.

Honey Chews

Drop Cookies
YIELD: *3 to 5 dozen*
TOTAL TIME: *35 minutes*

2 cups whole wheat flour
1 cup soy flour
1 cup rolled oats
¼ teaspoon salt
1 cup honey
1 cup canola oil
½ cup molasses
1 tablespoon fresh orange juice
½ teaspoon coffee liqueur
1 cup flaked coconut

1 Preheat the oven to 350 degrees. Lightly grease 2 baking sheets.

2 Combine the two flours, the oats, and salt.

3 In a large saucepan, combine the honey, oil, molasses, and orange juice and heat gently, stirring until well blended. Remove from the heat and stir in the coffee liqueur. Transfer to a large bowl, and gradually blend in the dry ingredients. Stir in the coconut.

4 Drop the dough by spoonfuls 1½ inches apart onto the prepared baking sheets.

5 Bake for 10 to 12 minutes, until lightly colored. Transfer to wire racks to cool.

Honey Chocolate Chips

Drop Cookies

YIELD: *4 to 5 dozen*
TOTAL TIME: *30 minutes*

1 cup all-purpose flour
¼ cup walnuts, ground fine
1 teaspoon baking powder
¼ teaspoon salt
½ cup vegetable shortening
½ cup honey
1 large egg
½ teaspoon crème de cacao
½ cup semisweet chocolate chips

1 Preheat the oven to 375 degrees.

2 Combine the flour, walnuts, baking powder, and salt.

3 In a large saucepan, melt the vegetable shortening with the honey, stirring until smooth. Remove from the heat and beat in the egg. Beat in the crème de cacao. Gradually blend in the dry ingredients. Stir in the chocolate chips.

4 Drop the dough by spoonfuls 1½ inches apart onto the prepared baking sheets.

5 Bake for 10 to 12 minutes, until lightly colored. Transfer to wire racks to cool.

Jelly Cookies

Formed Cookies

YIELD: *3 to 4 dozen*
TOTAL TIME: *45 minutes*

1 cup vegetable shortening
½ cup granulated sugar
1 large egg
1 teaspoon vanilla extract
½ teaspoon fresh lemon juice
2½ cups all-purpose flour
About ¼ to ½ cup grape jelly

1 Preheat the oven to 350 degrees. Lightly grease 2 baking sheets.

2 In a large bowl, cream the vegetable shortening and sugar. Beat in the egg. Beat in the vanilla extract and lemon juice. Gradually blend in the flour.

3 Pinch off walnut-sized pieces of the dough and roll into balls. Place 1 inch apart on the prepared baking sheets. Press your finger into the center of each cookie to make an indentation. Fill each cookie with a little jelly.

4 Bake for 20 to 25 minutes, until lightly colored. Transfer to wire racks to cool.

Jumbles II

Formed Cookies
YIELD: *3 to 4 dozen*
TOTAL TIME: *45 minutes*

½ cup vegetable shortening
1 cup granulated sugar
4 large eggs
2 tablespoons heavy cream
3 cups all-purpose flour

1 Preheat the oven to 350 degrees.

2 In a large bowl, cream the vegetable shortening and sugar. Beat in the eggs one at a time. Beat in the cream. Gradually blend in the flour.

3 Pinch off walnut-sized pieces of the dough and roll into pencil-thin ropes about 6 inches long. Form the ropes into horseshoes on ungreased baking sheets, placing them about 1 inch apart.

4 Bake for 12 to 15 minutes, until lightly colored. Transfer to wire racks to cool.

Baking notes: You can also twist 2 ropes together for each cookie and lay them out straight or form them into knots, circles, and other shapes.

Jumbo Oatmeal Crunches

Drop Cookies
YIELD: *2 to 4 dozen*
TOTAL TIME: *30 minutes*

3 cups all-purpose flour
1 teaspoon baking soda
Pinch of ground mace
1 teaspoon salt
2 cups vegetable shortening
2½ cups packed light brown sugar
2 large eggs
½ cup milk
3½ cups rolled oats
1 cup raisins (optional)

1 Preheat the oven to 350 degrees.

2 Combine the flour, baking soda, mace, and salt.

3 In a large bowl, cream the vegetable shortening and brown sugar. Beat in the eggs. Beat in the milk. Gradually blend in the dry ingredients. Fold in the oats and the optional raisins.

4 Drop the dough by tablespoonfuls 3 inches apart onto ungreased baking sheets. With the back of a spoon, spread the dough into 2½-inch rounds.

5 Bake for 10 to 12 minutes, until lightly colored. Transfer to wire racks to cool.

Baking notes: Nutmeg can be used in place of the mace.

KENTUCKY COCONUT DROPS

Drop Cookies
YIELD: *3 to 4 dozen*
TOTAL TIME: *35 minutes*

3 large egg whites
½ cup powdered sugar
1 cup grated fresh or packaged
  coconut

1 Preheat the oven to 325 degrees. Line 2 baking sheets with parchment paper.

2 In a large bowl, beat the egg whites until foamy. Beat in the powdered sugar and continue beating until stiff peaks form. Fold in the coconut.

3 Drop the mixture by spoonfuls 1 inch apart onto the prepared baking sheets.

4 Bake for 12 to 15 minutes, or until the edges start to color. Cool on the baking sheets on wire racks.

KRINGLES

Formed Cookies
YIELD: *2 to 3 dozen*
TOTAL TIME: *40 minutes*
CHILLING TIME: *24 hours*

3 cups all-purpose flour
½ teaspoon salt
1 cup vegetable shortening
1 cup granulated sugar
1 large egg
2 hard-boiled large egg yolks,
  chopped
1 teaspoon vanilla extract
1 large egg white, beaten
Granulated sugar for sprinkling

1 Combine the flour and salt.

2 In a large bowl, cream the vegetable shortening and sugar. Beat in the egg and egg yolks. Beat in the vanilla extract. Gradually blend in the dry ingredients. Cover tightly and chill for 24 hours.

3 Preheat the oven to 350 degrees.

4 Pinch off pieces of dough and roll into pencil-thin ropes about 6 inches long. Form the ropes into pretzels on ungreased baking sheets, placing them 1 inch apart. Brush with the beaten egg white and sprinkle with granulated sugar.

5 Bake for 12 to 14 minutes, until lightly colored. Transfer to wire racks to cool.

Baking notes: Decorate the pretzels with white or Dark chocolate Frosting (see Pantry).

Lemon Wafers

Rolled Cookies

Yield: *4 to 5 dozen*
Total time: *35 minutes*
Chilling time: *4 hours*

1 cup vegetable shortening
1 cup granulated sugar
4 large egg yolks
2 tablespoons fresh lemon juice
1 tablespoon lemon extract
3 cups all-purpose flour
Orange- or yellow-colored sugar
  crystals for sprinkling

1 In a large bowl, cream the vegetable shortening and sugar. Beat in the egg yolks. Beat in the lemon juice and lemon extract. Gradually blend in the flour. Cover and chill for 4 hours.

2 Preheat the oven to 350 degrees. Lightly grease 2 baking sheets.

3 On a floured surface, roll out the dough to a thickness of ⅛ inch. Using a 1½-inch round cookie cutter, cut into rounds and place 1 inch apart on the prepared baking sheets. Sprinkle with colored sugar crystals.

4 Bake for 10 to 12 minutes, until lightly colored. Transfer to wire racks to cool.

Little Jewel Cookies

Formed Cookies

Yield: *2 to 3 dozen*
Total time: *30 minutes*

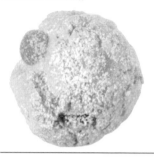

2 cups all-purpose flour
1 teaspoon salt
1 cup vegetable shortening
1 cup granulated sugar
1 cup packed light brown sugar
2 large eggs
1 teaspoon vanilla extract
1 teaspoon baking soda
1 tablespoon warm water
2 cups rolled oats
1 cup shredded coconut
1 cup gumdrops, chopped
Powdered sugar for rolling

1 Preheat the oven to 350 degrees. Lightly grease 2 baking sheets.

2 Combine the flour and salt.

3 In a large bowl, cream the vegetable shortening and sugars. Beat in the eggs one at a time. Beat in the vanilla extract.

4 Dissolve the baking soda in the warm water and add the egg mixture, beating until smooth. Gradually blend in the dry ingredients. Fold in the oats, coconut, and gumdrops.

5 Pinch off walnut-sized pieces of dough and roll into small balls. Place 1½ inches apart on the prepared baking sheets.

6 Bake for 10 to 12 minutes, until lightly colored. Transfer to wire racks to cool.

7 Roll the cooled cookies in powdered sugar.

Love Letters

Formed Cookies
Yield: 4 to 5 dozen
Total time: 40 minutes

Filling
2 large egg whites
¼ cup granulated sugar
½ teaspoon ground cinnamon
1 cup almonds, ground fine
1 teaspoon grated lemon zest
2 cups all-purpose flour
¼ teaspoon salt
¾ cup vegetable shortening
2 tablespoons granulated sugar
4 large egg yolks

1 Preheat the oven to 350 degrees.

2 To make the filling, in a medium bowl, beat the egg whites until stiff but not dry. Beat in the sugar and cinnamon. Fold in the almonds and lemon zest. Set aside.

3 Combine the flour and salt.

4 In a large bowl, cream the vegetable shortening and sugar. Beat in the egg yolks. Gradually blend in the dry ingredients.

5 On a floured surface, roll out the dough to a thickness of ¼ inch. Using a sharp knife, cut into 3-inch squares. Place 1 inch apart on ungreased baking sheets. Drop a teaspoonful of the filling into the center of each square and fold the corners into the center like an envelope. Lightly seal the seams.

6 Bake for 18 to 20 minutes, until lightly colored. Transfer to wire racks to cool.

Macadamia Nut Cookies

Drop Cookies
Yield: 2 to 3 dozen
Total time: 35 minutes
Chilling time: 4 hours

3 cups all-purpose flour
2 teaspoons baking soda
1 teaspoon salt
1½ cups vegetable shortening
1½ cups packed light brown sugar
⅔ cup granulated sugar
4 large eggs
1 teaspoon vanilla extract
1 teaspoon fresh lemon juice
2 cups macadamia nuts, chopped
½ cup rolled oats

1 Combine the flour, baking soda, and salt.

2 In a large bowl, cream the vegetable shortening and two sugars. Beat in the eggs one at a time, beating well after each addition. Beat in the vanilla extract and lemon juice. Gradually blend in the dry ingredients. Fold in the macadamia nuts and oats. Cover and chill for 4 hours.

3 Preheat the oven to 325 degrees. Lightly grease 2 baking sheets.

4 Drop the dough by spoonfuls 1½ inches apart onto the prepared baking sheets.

5 Bake for 15 to 18 minutes, until lightly colored. Transfer to wire racks to cool.

MACAROON NUT WAFERS

Drop Cookies

YIELD: *1 to 2 dozen*
TOTAL TIME: *35 minutes.*

2 large egg whites
¼ teaspoon salt
½ cup powdered sugar
1 teaspoon Amaretto
1 cup almonds, ground fine

1 Preheat the oven to 350 degrees. Line 2 baking sheets with parchment paper.

2 In a medium bowl, beat the egg whites with the salt until they form stiff peaks. Fold in the powdered sugar. Fold in the Amaretto. Fold in the almonds.

3 Drop the dough by spoonfuls 1½ inches apart onto the prepared baking sheets.

4 Bake for 15 to 20 minutes, until lightly colored. Cool slightly on the pans, then transfer to wire racks to cool completely.

MANDELBROT

Formed Cookies

YIELD: *3 to 4 dozen*
TOTAL TIME: *50 minutes*

3 cups all-purpose flour
1 teaspoon baking powder
¼ teaspoon salt
½ cup honey, warmed
6 tablespoons butter, at room
     temperature
3 large eggs
½ teaspoon grated lemon zest
½ cup pistachio nuts, chopped
1 teaspoon anise seeds, crushed

1 Preheat the oven to 350 degrees.

2 Combine the flour, baking powder, and salt.

3 In a large bowl, beat the honey and butter together. Beat in the eggs one at a time, beating well after each addition. Beat in the lemon zest. Gradually blend in the dry ingredients. Stir in the pistachio nuts and anise seeds.

4 Divide the dough in half. Shape each half into a loaf 12 inches long, 3 inches wide, and 1½–2 inches high. Place the logs on an ungreased baking sheet, leaving 1½ inches between them.

5 Bake for 25 to 30 minutes, until lightly colored and firm to the touch.

6 Transfer the loaves to a cutting board and cut into ½-inch-thick slices. Place 1 inch apart on the baking sheets and bake for 5 to 7 minutes longer, or until the slices are lightly toasted. Transfer to wire racks to cool.

Mexican Wedding Cakes

Formed Cookies

YIELD: *3 dozen*
TOTAL TIME: *45 minutes*

¾ cup vegetable shortening
¼ cup granulated sugar
1 teaspoon vanilla extract
2 cups all-purpose flour
½ cup walnuts, chopped
Powdered sugar for rolling

1 Preheat the oven to 200 degrees. Lightly grease 2 baking sheets.

2 In a large bowl, cream the shortening and sugar together. Beat in the vanilla extract. Gradually blend in the flour. Fold in the walnuts.

3 Pinch off walnut-sized pieces of dough and roll into balls. Place 1 inch apart on the prepared baking sheets.

4 Bake for 25 to 35 minutes, or until golden. Roll in powdered sugar and transfer to wire racks to cool.

Milaenderli

Rolled Cookies

YIELD: *3 to 4 dozen*
TOTAL TIME: *30 minutes*
CHILLING TIME: *1 hour*

2¾ cups all-purpose flour
⅛ teaspoon salt
¾ cup vegetable shortening
¾ cup granulated sugar
1 large egg
1 large egg yolk
½ teaspoon fresh lemon juice
½ teaspoon grated lemon zest
1 large egg yolk, beaten

1 Combine the flour and salt.

2 In a large bowl, cream the vegetable shortening and sugar. Beat in the egg and egg yolk. Beat in the lemon juice and zest. Gradually blend in the dry ingredients. Cover and chill for 1 hour.

3 Preheat the oven to 375 degrees. Lightly grease 2 baking sheets.

4 On a floured surface, roll out the dough to a thickness of ¼ inch. Using cookie cutters, cut into shapes and place 1 inch apart on the prepared baking sheets. Brush the beaten egg yolk over the top of the cookies.

5 Bake for 10 to 12 minutes, until lightly colored. Transfer to wire racks to cool.

Baking notes: Traditionally these Christmas cookies are cut into the shapes of reindeer and Christmas trees.

MINT CHOCOLATE COOKIES

Drop Cookies

YIELD: *3 to 4 dozen*
TOTAL TIME: *35 minutes*
CHILLING TIME: *4 hours*

3 cups all-purpose flour
1½ cups walnuts, ground
½ teaspoon baking soda
½ teaspoon salt
1 cup vegetable shortening
1 cup granulated sugar
½ cup packed light brown sugar
2 large eggs
1 teaspoon vanilla extract
14 ounces mint-chocolate wafer candies, such as After Eights or Andies, chopped

1 Combine the flour, walnuts, baking soda, and salt.

2 In a large bowl, cream the vegetable shortening and two sugars. Beat in the eggs. Beat in the vanilla extract. Gradually blend in the dry ingredients. Fold in the mint wafers. Cover and chill for 4 hours.

3 Preheat the oven to 350 degrees.

4 Drop the dough by spoonfuls 1½ inches apart onto ungreased baking sheets.

5 Bake for 10 to 12 minutes, until lightly colored. Transfer to wire racks to cool.

Baking notes: For a stronger mint flavor, add 2 drops of peppermint oil. Instead of chocolate mint wafers, you can use mint-flavored chocolate chips, or grated chocolate and a teaspoon of mint extract.

MINT COOKIES

Drop Cookies

YIELD: *4 to 5 dozen*
TOTAL TIME: *30 minutes*
CHILLING TIME: *4 hours*

3 cups all-purpose flour
½ teaspoon salt
1 cup vegetable shortening
1 cup granulated sugar
1 cup packed light brown sugar
2 large eggs
2 tablespoons water
1 teaspoon vanilla extract
1 pound small chocolate mint candies

1 Combine the flour and salt.

2 In a large bowl, cream the vegetable shortening and two sugars. Beat in the eggs. Beat in the water and vanilla extract. Gradually blend in the dry ingredients. Cover and chill for 4 hours.

3 Preheat the oven to 350 degrees. Lightly grease 2 baking sheets.

4 Drop the dough by spoonfuls 1½ inches apart onto the prepared baking sheets. Press a chocolate mint into the center of each cookie so it is standing on its edge.

5 Bake for 10 to 12 minutes, until lightly colored. Transfer to wire racks to cool.

MOLASSES COOKIES

Rolled Cookies

YIELD: *6 to 7 dozen*
TOTAL TIME: *40 minutes*

5 cups all-purpose flour
1½ cups whole wheat flour
1 cup rice flour
2 teaspoons baking powder
2 teaspoons baking soda
2 teaspoons ground cinnamon
2 teaspoons ground ginger
½ teaspoon salt
2 cups vegetable shortening
2 cups granulated sugar
3 large eggs
2 cups molasses
1½ cups hot water

1 Preheat the oven to 350 degrees. Lightly grease 2 baking sheets.

2 Combine the three flours, the baking powder, baking soda, spices, and salt.

3 In a large bowl, cream the vegetable shortening and sugar. Beat in the eggs. Beat in the molasses. Beat in the hot water. Gradually blend in the dry ingredients.

4 On a floured surface, roll out the dough to a thickness of ¼ inch. Using a 2½-inch round cookie cutter, cut out cookies an place 1 inch apart on the prepared baking sheets.

5 Bake for 10 to 15 minutes, until lightly colored. Transfer to wire racks to cool.

NUT COOKIES

Drop Cookies

YIELD: *1 to 2 dozen*
TOTAL TIME: *35 minutes*

¾ cup all-purpose flour
1 teaspoon baking powder
¼ cup butter, at room temperature
¼ cup vegetable shortening
½ cup granulated sugar
2 large eggs
1 teaspoon vanilla extract
¾ cup walnuts, chopped

1 Preheat the oven to 350 degrees.

2 Combine the flour and baking powder.

3 In a large bowl, cream the butter, vegetable shortening, and sugar. Beat in the eggs. Beat in the vanilla extract. Gradually blend in the dry ingredients.

4 Drop the dough by spoonfuls 1½ inches apart onto ungreased baking sheets. Sprinkle with chopped nuts.

5 Bake for 10 to 12 minutes, until lightly colored. Transfer to wire racks to cool.

NEW YEAR'S EVE PRETZELS

Formed Cookies

YIELD: *7 to 9 dozen*
TOTAL TIME: *45 minutes*
RISING TIME: *2 hours*

2 cups milk
½ cup granulated sugar
6 cups all-purpose flour
2 tablespoons active dry yeast
½ cup butter, at room temperature
3 large eggs

ICING
1 cup powdered sugar
1 tablespoon water
1 tablespoon vanilla extract
¼ cup chopped nuts

1 In a large saucepan, heat the milk just until warm (105 degrees); do not overheat. Remove fom the heat and stir in the sugar. Stir in 1 cup of the flour and the yeast. Blend in the butter. Stir in the eggs one at a time, blending well after each addition. Then blend in the remaining flour, ¼ cup at a time until a soft dough forms.

2 Turn the dough out onto a floured surface and knead for 5 minutes, or until smooth. Place in a large bowl, cover with a clean cloth, and let rise in a warm place for 1 hour, or until doubled in bulk.

3 Punch down the dough and knead briefly. Let rise for a second time.

4 Preheat the oven to 375 degrees. Lightly grease 2 baking sheets.

5 Punch down the dough. Pinch off large pieces and roll into ropes about 30 inches long. Cut smaller ropes, approximately 3 to 4 inches to make the pretzels. Form the ropes into pretzel shapes on the prepared baking sheets, placing them 1½ inches apart. Cover and let rest for 10 to 15 minutes.

6 Bake for 25 to 30 minutes, until golden brown. Transfer to wire racks to cool.

7 To make the icing, combine the powdered sugar, water, and vanilla extract in a bowl and stir until smooth. Stir in the nuts.

8 Spread the icing over the tops of the cooled pretzels.

Baking notes: These are the soft-crust pretzels that are so popular. The pretzels can be as big or as small as you want.

OATMEAL-COCONUT CRISPS

Drop Cookies

YIELD: *4 to 5 dozen*
TOTAL TIME: *30 minutes*

1 cup all-purpose flour
1 teaspoon baking powder
½ teaspoon baking soda
¼ teaspoon salt
¾ cup vegetable shortening
1⅔ cups granulated sugar
2 large eggs
1½ teaspoons vanilla extract
2½ cups rolled oats
1 cup flaked coconut

1 Preheat the oven to 375 degrees. Lightly grease 2 baking sheets.

2 Combine the flour, baking powder, baking soda, and salt.

3 In a large bowl, cream the vegetable shortening and sugar. Beat in the eggs. Beat in the vanilla. Gradually blend in the dry ingredients. Fold in the oats and coconut.

4 Drop the dough by spoonfuls 3 inches apart onto the prepared baking sheets.

5 Bake for 12 to 14 minutes, until golden brown. Transfer to wire racks to cool.

OATMEAL CRISPS

Drop Cookies

YIELD: *2 to 3 dozen*
TOTAL TIME: *30 minutes*

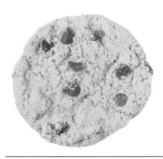

1¼ cups all-purpose flour
½ teaspoon baking powder
½ teaspoon baking soda
½ teaspoon salt
1 cup vegetable shortening
¼ cup granulated sugar
1 cup packed light brown sugar
2 large eggs
¼ teaspoon milk
1 teaspoon vanilla extract
3 cups rolled oats
1 cup (6 ounces) chocolate chips (see Baking notes)

1 Preheat the oven to 350 degrees.

2 Combine the flour, baking powder, baking soda, and salt.

3 In a large bowl, cream the vegetable shortening and two sugars. Beat in the eggs. Beat in the milk and vanilla extract. Gradually blend in the dry ingredients. Fold in the oats and chocolate chips.

4 Drop the dough by spoonfuls 1½ inches apart onto ungreased baking sheets.

5 Bake for 10 to 12 minutes, until lightly colored. Transfer to wire racks to cool.

Baking notes: You can use semi-sweet chocolate, milk chocolate, or butterscotch chips. If making these for kids, omit the chips and press several M & Ms into the top of each cookie.

OATMEAL THINS

Drop Cookies

YIELD: *2 to 3 dozen*
TOTAL TIME: *30 minutes*

1 cup rolled oats
2 teaspoons baking powder
½ teaspoon salt
1 tablespoon vegetable shortening
1 cup granulated sugar
2 large eggs
1 teaspoon vanilla extract

1 Preheat the oven to 350 degrees. Lightly grease 2 baking sheets.

2 Combine the oats, baking powder, and salt.

3 In a large bowl, cream the shortening and sugar. Beat in the eggs. Beat in the vanilla extract. Gradually blend in the dry ingredients.

4 Drop the dough by spoonfuls 2 inches apart onto the prepared baking sheets.

5 Bake for 12 to 15 minutes, until lightly colored. Transfer to wire racks to cool.

Baking notes: Keep a close eye on these cookies; they burn very easily.

OLD-FASHIONED COOKIES

Rolled Cookies

YIELD: *5 to 6 dozen*
TOTAL TIME: *30 minutes*

3½ cups all-purpose flour
2½ teaspoons baking powder
½ teaspoon salt
1 cup vegetable shortening
1½ cups granulated sugar
2 large eggs
1 tablespoon rum
Vanilla Icing (see Pantry)

1 Preheat the oven to 350 degrees.

2 Combine the flour, baking powder, and salt.

3 In a large bowl, cream the vegetable shortening and sugar. Beat in the eggs. Beat in the rum. Gradually blend in the dry ingredients.

4 On a floured surface, roll out the dough to a thickness of ¼ inch. Using a 2-inch round cookie cutter, cut out cookies and place 1 inch apart on ungreased baking sheets.

5 Bake for 10 to 12 minutes, until lightly colored and firm to the touch. Transfer to wire racks to cool.

6 Drizzle the icing over the cooled cookies.

Baking notes: You can decorate these cookies with gum drops or small candies—be creative.

OLD-FASHIONED SOFT GINGER COOKIES

Rolled Cookies

YIELD: *4 to 5 dozen*
TOTAL TIME: *35 minutes*
CHILLING TIME: *6 hours*

4 cups all-purpose flour
2 teaspoons baking soda
1 tablespoon ground ginger
1 teaspoon salt
¾ cups vegetable shortening
2 cups packed light brown sugar
⅔ cup molasses
⅔ cup boiling water

1 Combine the flour, baking soda, ginger, and salt.

2 In a large bowl, cream the vegetable shortening and brown sugar. Add in the molasses and boiling water, beating until smooth. Gradually blend in the dry ingredients. Cover and chill for at least 6 hours.

3 Preheat the oven to 350 degrees. Lightly grease 2 baking sheets.

4 On a floured surface, roll out the dough to a thickness of ¼ inch. Using a 2-inch round cookie cutter, cut the cookies and place 1 inch apart on the prepared baking sheets.

5 Bake for 18 to 20 minutes, until lightly colored. Transfer to wire racks to cool.

Baking notes: These cookies may be iced once cool. Store tightly covered to retain their flavor and softness; should the cookies become hard, place half an apple in the cookie container for 8 hours to soften them.

ORANGE-PECAN COOKIES

Drop Cookies

YIELD: *3 to 5 dozen*
TOTAL TIME: *35 minutes*

1 cup all-purpose flour
¼ teaspoon baking powder
¼ teaspoon salt
¼ cup vegetable shortening
1 cup granulated sugar
1 large egg
6 tablespoons fresh orange juice
2 tablespoons orange liqueur
¼ cup pecans, chopped fine

1 Preheat the oven to 375 degrees. Lightly grease 2 baking sheets.

2 Combine the flour, baking powder, and salt.

3 In a large bowl, cream the vegetable shortening and sugar. Beat in the egg. Beat in the orange juice and orange liqueur. Gradually blend in the dry ingredients. Stir in the pecans.

4 Drop the dough by spoonfuls 1½ inches apart onto the prepared baking sheets.

5 Bake for 12 to 15 minutes, until lightly colored. Transfer to wire racks to cool.

Orange-Raisin Cookies

Drop Cookies

YIELD: *4 to 5 dozen*
TOTAL TIME: *30 minutes*

1 cup all-purpose flour
1 teaspoon baking soda
½ teaspoon salt
1 cup vegetable shortening
1 cup granulated sugar
1 cup packed light brown sugar
2 large eggs
¼ cup frozen orange juice concentrate, thawed
2 teaspoons orange liqueur
1 cup rolled oats
¾ cup golden raisins

1 Preheat the oven to 350 degrees. Lightly grease 2 baking sheets.

2 Combine the flour, baking soda, and salt.

3 In a large bowl, cream the vegetable shortening and two sugars. Beat in the eggs. Beat in the orange juice concentrate and liqueur. Gradually blend in the dry ingredients. Fold in the oats and raisins.

4 Drop the dough by spoonfuls 2 inches apart onto the prepared baking sheets.

5 Bake for 12 to 14 minutes, until lightly colored. Transfer to wire racks to cool.

Baking notes: Half a cup of chopped nuts (any kind) can be added to the dough.

Pastiniai Natale

Rolled Cookies

YIELD: *2 to 4 dozen*
TOTAL TIME: *30 minutes*
CHILLING TIME: *4 hours*

3 cups all-purpose flour
1 tablespoon baking powder
¼ teaspoon salt
1 tablespoon lemon zest, grated
1 cup vegetable shortening
1 cup granulated sugar
2 large eggs
¼ cup pistachio nuts, chopped
Lemon Glaze (see Pantry)
Chopped pistachio nuts for sprinkling

1 Combine the flour, baking powder, and salt.

2 In a large bowl, cream the vegetable shortening and sugar. Beat in the eggs. Gradually blend in the dry ingredients. Fold in the lemon zest. Fold in the pistachio nuts. Cover and chill for 4 hours.

3 Preheat the oven to 325 degrees. Lightly grease 2 baking sheets.

4 On a floured surface, roll out the dough to a thickness of ¼ inch. Using a 2-inch round cookie cutter, cut out the cookies and place 1 inch apart on the prepared baking sheets.

5 Bake for 8 to 10 minutes, until lightly colored. Transfer to wire racks to cool.

6 Ice the cooled cookies with the lemon glaze and sprinkle chopped pistachio nuts over the tops.

Peanut Butter Cookies

Formed Cookies

YIELD: *2 to 3 dozen*
TOTAL TIME: *30 minutes*

1½ cups all-purpose flour
1½ teaspoons baking powder
½ teaspoon salt
1 cup packed light brown sugar
½ cup peanut butter
¼ cup vegetable shortening
1 large egg
2 tablespoons fresh orange juice
1½ teaspoons vanilla extract
1½ tablespoons grated orange zest
¾ cup currants

1 Preheat the oven to 400 degrees. Lightly grease 2 baking sheets.

2 Combine the flour, baking powder, and salt.

3 In a large bowl, beat together the sugar, peanut butter, and vegetable shortening until smooth and creamy. Beat in the egg. Beat in the orange juice and vanilla extract. Beat in the orange zest. Gradually blend in the dry ingredients. Stir in the currants.

4 Pinch off walnut-sized pieces of the dough and roll into small balls. Place 2 inches apart on the prepared baking sheets. Flatten each ball with the back of a fork dipped in flour, making a criss-cross pattern.

5 Bake for 12 to 15 minutes, until golden brown. Transfer to wire racks to cool.

Baking notes: These taste even better if allowed to age for 1 day.

Peanut Butter Jumbo Cookies

Drop Cookies

YIELD: *2 to 3 dozen*
TOTAL TIME: *30 minutes*

2½ cups all-purpose flour
1 teaspoon baking powder
1½ teaspoons baking soda
2 cups packed light brown sugar
1 cup vegetable shortening
1 cup peanut butter
2 large eggs

1 Preheat the oven to 350 degrees. Lightly grease 2 baking sheets.

2 Combine the flour, baking powder, and baking soda.

3 In a large bowl, beat together the brown sugar, vegetable shortening, peanut butter, and eggs. Gradually blend in the dry ingredients. The dough will be very soft.

4 Using a serving spoon, drop the dough by spoonfuls 3 inches apart onto the prepared baking sheets. Using the back of a spoon dipped in flour, spread the cookies into large rounds.

5 Bake for 10 to 12 minutes, until golden brown. Cool on the baking sheets on wire racks.

Baking notes: Chunky peanut butter can be used for more crunch.

Pecan Crispies

Formed Cookies

Yield: *2 to 3 dozen*
Total time: *30 minutes*
Chilling time: *4 hours*

2 cups all-purpose flour
2 teaspoons baking powder
½ teaspoon salt
1½ cups vegetable shortening
1 cup granulated sugar
2 large eggs
1 teaspoon vanilla extract
¾ cup pecans, chopped
Powdered sugar

1 Combine the flour, baking powder, and salt.

2 In a large bowl, cream the vegetable shortening and sugar. Beat in the eggs. Beat in the vanilla extract. Gradually blend in the dry ingredients. If the dough seems too dry, add a little water ½ teaspoonful at a time. Cover and chill for 4 hours.

3 Preheat the oven to 350 degrees.

4 Pinch off walnut-sized pieces of the dough and roll into balls. Roll in the chopped pecans and place 1½ inches apart on ungreased baking sheets. Flatten each ball with the bottom of a glass dipped in powdered sugar.

5 Bake for 6 to 8 minutes, until lightly colored. Cool slightly on the baking sheets, then transfer to wire racks to cool completely.

Pepparkakor

Rolled Cookies

Yield: *6 to 7 dozen*
Total time: *30 minutes*
Chilling time: *24 hours*

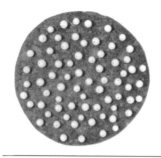

1⅔ cups all-purpose flour
½ teaspoon baking soda
¾ teaspoon ground ginger
½ teaspoon ground cinnamon
¼ teaspoon ground cloves
¼ teaspoon ground cardamom
½ teaspoon salt
6 tablespoons butter, at room temperature
⅓ cup granulated sugar
¼ cup molasses
1 teaspoon grated orange zest
¼ cup almonds, chopped

1 Combine the flour, baking soda, spices, and salt.

2 In a large bowl, cream the butter and sugar. Beat in the molasses. Beat in the orange zest. Gradually blend in the dry ingredients. Fold in the almonds. Cover and chill for 24 hours.

3 Preheat the oven to 350 degrees. Lightly grease 2 baking sheets.

4 On a floured surface, roll out the dough to a thickness of ⅛ inch. Using cookie cutters, cut into shapes and place the cookies 1 inch apart on the prepared baking sheets.

5 Bake for 5 to 7 minutes, until lightly colored. Transfer to wire racks to cool.

Baking notes: These can be decorated with Vanilla Icing (see Pantry).

Pepper Cookies

Rolled Cookies

YIELD: *3 to 4 dozen*
TOTAL TIME: *30 minutes*
CHILLING TIME: *8 hours*

2½ cups all-purpose flour
¼ cup almonds, ground fine
1 teaspoon baking soda
1 teaspoon ground cinnamon
1 teaspoon ground cardamom
1 teaspoon ground ginger
½ teaspoon ground allspice
½ teaspoon salt
1 cup vegetable shortening
1 cup granulated sugar
1 large egg
½ cup corn syrup
Vanilla Icing (see Pantry)

1 Combine the flour, almonds, baking soda, spices, and salt.

2 In a large bowl, cream the vegetable shortening and sugar. Beat in the egg. Beat in the corn syrup. Gradually blend in the dry ingredients. Cover and chill for 8 hours.

3 Preheat the oven to 350 degrees.

4 On a floured surface, roll out the dough to a thickness of ¼ inch. Using cookie cutters, cut into shapes and place 1 inch apart on ungreased baking sheets.

5 Bake for 8 to 10 minutes, until lightly colored. Transfer to wire racks to cool.

6 Frost with the icing when cool.

Peppermint Delights

Rolled Cookies

YIELD: *4 to 5 dozen*
TOTAL TIME: *30 minutes*

1½ cups all-purpose flour
½ teaspoon salt
1 cup vegetable shortening
1 cup powdered sugar
2 teaspoons vanilla extract
1 cup rolled oats
¼ cup crushed peppermint candies

1 Preheat the oven to 325 degrees.

2 Combine the flour and salt.

3 In a large bowl, cream the vegetable shortening and powdered sugar. Beat in the vanilla extract. Gradually blend in the dry ingredients. Fold in the oats. Fold in the candies.

4 On a floured surface, roll out the dough to a thickness of ¼ inch. Using a 1½-inch round cookie cutter, cut out the cookies and place 1 inch apart on ungreased baking sheets.

5 Bake for 10 to 12 minutes, until lightly colored. Transfer to wire racks to cool.

Baking notes: Be sure to crush the candy very fine. For a festive look, add a few drops of red food coloring to the dough.

Peppermint Meringues

Formed Cookies

Yield: *2 to 3 dozen*
Total time: *45 minutes*

3 large egg whites
¾ cup granulated sugar
¾ teaspoon cider vinegar
6 drops peppermint oil
Green food coloring (optional)

1 Preheat the oven to 200 degrees. Line 2 baking sheets with parchment paper.

2 In a large bowl, beat the egg whites until foamy. Gradually beat in the sugar and beat until the whites hold stiff peaks. Fold in the vinegar and peppermint oil. Fold in the optional food coloring and beat for 5 minutes longer.

3 Place the mixture in a cookie press or a pastry bag fitted with a star tip and press or pipe out 1-inch mounds onto the prepared baking sheets, spacing them 1 inch apart.

4 Bake for 30 to 35 minutes, until firm to the touch. Cool on the baking pans on a wire racks.

Petticoat Tails

Formed Cookies

Yield: *3 to 4 dozen*
Total time: *30 minutes*

3 cups all-purpose flour
½ teaspoon baking powder
1 cup butter, at room temperature
½ cup granulated sugar
1 tablespoon heavy cream
1 teaspoon vanilla extract

1 Preheat the oven to 350 degrees. Lightly grease 2 baking sheets.

2 Combine the flour and baking powder.

3 In a large bowl, cream the butter and sugar. Beat in the heavy cream and vanilla extract. Gradually blend in the dry ingredients.

4 Turn the dough out onto a floured surface and knead until smooth.

5 Divide the dough into 6 equal pieces. Roll each piece into ¼-inch-thick round. Using a 1½-inch-round cookie cutter, cut out the centers of the rounds. Cut each round into 6 to 8 wedges. Carefully place the wedges 1 inch apart on the prepared baking sheets. Prick all over with the tines of a fork.

6 Bake for 12 to 15 minutes, until lightly colored. Cool slightly on the baking sheet, then transfer to wire racks to cool completely.

Baking notes: You can frost these with a thin layer of Vanilla Icing (see Pantry). This cookie was created for Queen Victoria.

PFEFFERNÜSSE

Rolled Cookies

YIELD: *4 to 5 dozen*
TOTAL TIME: *30 minutes*
CHILLING TIME: *4 hours*
RESTING TIME: *4 hours*

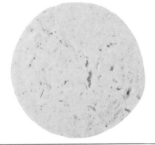

3 cups all-purpose flour
1 teaspoon baking powder
½ teaspoon ground cinnamon
¼ teaspoon ground nutmeg
¼ teaspoon ground cloves
¼ teaspoon salt
1 cup granulated sugar
3 large eggs
1½ tablespoons fresh lemon juice
1 teaspoon hazelnut syrup (optional)
½ teaspoon grated lemon zest
¼ cup hazelnuts, chopped
About 1 teaspoon brandy

1 Combine the flour, baking powder, spices, and salt.

2 In a large bowl, beat the sugar and eggs until thick and light-colored. Beat in the lemon juice and hazelnut syrup. Beat in the lemon zest. Gradually blend in the dry ingredients. Stir in the hazelnuts. Cover and chill for 4 hours.

3 Lightly grease 2 baking sheets. the flour. Fold in the blueberries. Spread the mixture evenly in the prepared baking pan.

4 Bake for 20 to 25 minutes, until lightly colored on top and firm to the touch. Cool in the pan on a wire rack before cutting into large or small bars.

PUMPKIN COOKIES

Drop Cookies

YIELD: *3 to 5 dozen*
TOTAL TIME: *30 minutes*

1½ cups all-purpose flour
¾ teaspoon baking powder
¼ teaspoon baking soda
1 teaspoon ground allspice
⅓ cup vegetable shortening
1 cup solid-pack pumpkin
1 large egg
1 cup dates, pitted and chopped
Pecan halves for decorating

1 Preheat the oven to 350 degrees. Lightly grease 2 baking sheets.

2 Combine the flour, baking powder, baking soda, allspice.

3 In a large bowl, beat the vegetable shortening and pumpkin pulp until smooth. Beat in the egg. Gradually blend in the dry ingredients. Stir in the dates.

4 Drop the dough by spoonfuls 1½ inches apart onto the prepared baking sheets. Push a pecan half into the center of each cookie.

5 Bake for 8 to 10 minutes, until lightly colored. Transfer to wire racks to cool.

Pure Fruit Cookies

Drop Cookies

YIELD: *2 to 3 dozen*
TOTAL TIME: *35 minutes*

1½ cups rolled oats
½ cup oat bran cereal
¼ teaspoon salt
⅓ cup canola oil
3 mashed bananas
1 teaspoon vanilla extract
1½ cups dried apricots, chopped
½ cup almonds, chopped fine

1 Preheat the oven to 350 degrees. Lightly grease 2 baking sheets.

2 Combine the oats, oat bran cereal, and salt.

3 In a large bowl, beat the oil, bananas, and vanilla extract until smooth. Gradually blend in the dry ingredients. Stir in the apricots and almonds.

4 Drop the dough by spoonfuls 1½ inches apart onto the prepared baking sheets.

5 Bake for 20 to 25 minutes, or until lightly colored. Transfer to wire racks to cool

Queen Elizabeth Cookies

Rolled Cookies

YIELD: *2 to 3 dozen*
TOTAL TIME: *30 minutes*

3 cups all-purpose flour
1 teaspoon baking powder
1 tablespoon vegetable shortening
¾ cup granulated sugar
2 large eggs
½ teaspoon fresh orange juice
Candied citron cut into thin strips

1 Preheat the oven to 350 degrees. Lightly grease 2 baking sheets.

2 Combine the flour and baking powder.

3 In a large bowl, cream the vegetable shortening and sugar. Beat in the eggs one at a time. Beat in the orange juice. Gradually blend in the dry ingredients.

4 On a floured surface, roll out the dough to a thickness of ¼ inch. Using a 2-inch round cookie cutter, cut out cookies and place 1½ inches apart on the prepared baking sheets. Lay a strip of citron across each cookie.

5 Bake for 15 to 18 minutes, until lightly colored. Transfer to wire racks to cool.

Baking notes: Recipes for this cookie first appeared around the time of the coronation of Queen Elizabeth II.

QUEEN VICTORIA BISCUITS

Rolled Cookies
YIELD: *4 to 5 dozen*
TOTAL TIME: *30 minutes*

4 cups rolled oats
1 teaspoon ground cinnamon
¼ teaspoon ground nutmeg
1 cup vegetable shortening
1 cup powdered sugar
1 cup currants

1 Grind oats finely in a food a food processor.

2 Preheat the oven to 350 degrees. Lightly grease 2 baking sheets.

3 Combine the oats, currants, cinnamon, and nutmeg.

4 In a large bowl, cream the vegetable shortening and powdered sugar. Gradually blend in the dry ingredients. Fold in the currants. If the dough seem very dry, add a little water a teaspoonful at a time.

5 On a floured surface, roll out the dough to a thickness of ½ inch. Using a 1½-inch round cookie cutter, cut out cookies and place 1 inch apart on the prepared baking sheets.

6 Bake for 15 to 18 minutes, or until lightly colored. Transfer to wire racks to cool.

RAISIN BRAN COOKIES

Drop Cookies
YIELD: *3 to 5 dozen*
TOTAL TIME: *30 minutes*

1 cup raisin bran
½ cup granulated sugar
1 apple, peeled, cored, and grated
½ cup milk
1 teaspoon vanilla extract

1 Preheat the oven to 350 degrees. Lightly grease 2 baking sheets.

2 In a large bowl, combine the raisin bran, sugar, and apple. Stir in the milk and vanilla extract and mix well.

3 Drop the dough by spoonfuls 1 inch apart onto the prepared baking sheets.

4 Bake for 12 to 15 minutes, until lightly colored. Transfer to wire racks to cool.

RAISIN COOKIES

Drop Cookies

YIELD: *4 to 5 dozen*
TOTAL TIME: *30 minutes*

3 cups all-purpose flour
2 teaspoons baking soda
½ teaspoon ground cloves
½ teaspoon ground cinnamon
½ teaspoon salt
1 cup vegetable shortening
2 cups packed light brown sugar
2 large eggs
1 cup sour milk
1 cup walnuts, chopped
½ cup raisins
½ cup golden raisins

1 Preheat the oven to 350 degrees.

2 Combine the flour, baking soda, spices, and salt.

3 In a large bowl, cream the vegetable shortening and brown sugar. Beat in the eggs. Beat in the sour milk. Gradually blend in the dry ingredients. Stir in the walnuts and raisins.

4 Drop the dough by spoonfuls 1½ inches apart onto ungreased baking sheets.

5 Bake for 9 to 12 minutes, until lightly colored. Transfer to wire racks to cool.

RUFFLES

Drop Cookies

YIELD: *2 to 3 dozen*
TOTAL TIME: *30 minutes*

2 large egg whites
2 cups powdered sugar
1 cup pecans, chopped
1 cup almonds, chopped
1 teaspoon distilled white vinegar
1 teaspoon almond extract

1 Preheat the oven to 300 degrees. Lightly grease baking sheets.

2 In a medium bowl, with an electric beater beat the egg whites until they hold soft peaks. Gradually beat in the powdered sugar and beat until stiff peaks form. Fold in the two nuts, vinegar, and almond extract.

3 Drop the dough by spoonfuls 1½ inches apart onto the prepared baking sheets.

4 Bake for 12 to 15 minutes, or until lightly colored. Transfer the cookies to wire racks to cool.

RUGELACH

Rolled Cookies

YIELD: *2 to 3 dozen*
TOTAL TIME: *40 minutes*
CHILLING TIME: *4 hours*

1 cup butter, at room temperature
8 ounces cream cheese, at room
   temperature
6 tablespoons powdered sugar
1 tablespoon raspberry-flavored
   brandy
2¾ cups all-purpose flour

FILLING
¾ cup packed light brown sugar
½ cup almonds, chopped
½ cup raisins, plumped in warm
   water and drained
1 teaspoon ground cinnamon

1 Combine the butter, cream cheese, and powdered sugar in a large bowl and beat until smooth and creamy. Beat in the brandy. Gradually blend in the flour. Divide the dough into 4 pieces. Wrap the dough in waxed paper and chill for 4 hours.

2 Preheat the oven to 350 degrees. Lightly grease 2 baking sheets.

3 To make the filling, combine all the ingredients in a small bowl and toss to mix.

4 On a floured surface, roll out each piece of dough into a 9-inch circle. Spread one-quarter of the filling over each round. Cut each round into 8 wedges. Starting at the wide end, roll up each wedge. Place 1 inch apart on the prepared baking sheets, curving the ends to form crescents.

5 Bake for 20 to 25 minutes, until lightly colored. Transfer to wire racks to cool.

RUM BALLS

Formed Cookies

YIELD: *3 to 5 dozen*
TOTAL TIME: *30 minutes*
AGING TIME: *1 week*

2½ cups crushed gingersnaps
½ cup honey
6 tablespoons rum
1½ cups pecans, ground fine
Powdered sugar for rolling

1 In a large bowl, combine all of the ingredients and stir to form a sticky dough. Pinch off small pieces of dough and roll into balls. Roll each ball in powdered sugar.

2 Store in an airtight container for at least 1 week before serving. Before serving, roll the balls a second time in powdered sugar.

Baking notes: These cookies are not for children.

Rum-Topped Ginger Cookies

Rolled Cookies

YIELD: *3 to 4 dozen*
TOTAL TIME: *45 minutes*
CHILLING TIME: *30 minutes*

2 cups all-purpose flour
⅔ cup granulated sugar
2 teaspoons ground ginger
Pinch of salt
½ cup butter, chilled and cut into small pieces
½ cup large-curd cottage cheese
1 large egg white, beaten with 2 teaspoons water for egg glaze
Colored sugar crystals

TOPPING

1½ cups butter, at room temperature
3 cups powdered sugar
1 tablespoon minced crystallized ginger
3 tablespoons rum

1 Preheat oven to 350 degrees. Lightly grease 2 baking sheets.

2 In a large bowl, combine the flour, sugar, ginger, and salt. Cut in the butter until the mixture resembles coarse crumbs. Blend in the cottage cheese. The dough will be stiff. If the dough is too dry, add a little water 1 teaspoon at a time. Cover and chill for 30 minutes.

3 On a floured surface, roll out dough to a thickness of ⅛ inch. Using a 2-inch round or 2-inch scalloped cookie cutter, cut out cookies. Place 1 inch apart on the prepared baking sheets and brush with egg glaze. Sprinkle with the sugar crystals.

4 Bake for 10 to 12 minutes, or until browned around the edges. Transfer to wire racks to cool.

5 To make the topping, cream the butter and sugar in a small bowl. Beat in the ginger and rum. Spread over the top of the cooled cookies.

Baking notes: The ginger flavor will be more intense if the cookies are stored in an airtight container to age.

Rum Cookies

Drop Cookies

Yield: *6 to 8 dozen*
Total time: *30 minutes*
Chilling time: *4 hours*

2 cups all-purpose flour
2 teaspoons baking powder
½ teaspoon salt
1 cup butter, at room temperature
1 cup packed light brown sugar
3 large eggs
½ cup rum
1 teaspoon almond extract

1 Combine the flour, baking powder, and salt.

2 In a large bowl, cream the butter and sugar. Beat in the eggs. Beat in the rum and almond extract. Gradually blend in the dry ingredients. Cover and chill for 4 hours.

3 Preheat the oven to 400 degrees.

4 Drop the dough by spoonfuls 1½ inches apart onto the prepared baking sheets.

5 Bake for 6 to 8 minutes, until lightly colored. Transfer to wire racks to cool.

Russian Tea Biscuits I

Formed Cookies

Yield: *3 to 6 dozen*
Total time: *35 minutes*

2¼ cups all-purpose flour
¼ teaspoon salt
1 cup butter, at room temperature
¾ cup powdered sugar
1 teaspoon vodka
¾ cup hazelnuts, chopped fine
Powdered sugar for sprinkling

1 Preheat the oven to 325 degrees.

2 Combine the flour and salt.

3 In a large bowl, cream the butter and powdered sugar. Beat in the vodka. Gradually blend in the dry ingredients. Fold in the hazelnuts.

4 Pinch off walnut-sized pieces of dough and roll into balls. Place 1½ inches apart on ungreased baking sheets. Flatten each ball with the bottom of a glass dipped in flour.

5 Bake for 12 to 15 minutes, until lightly colored. Sprinkle with powdered sugar and transfer to wire racks to cool

Russian Tea Biscuits II

Formed Cookies

Yield: *4 to 5 dozen*
Total time: *30 minutes*

2¼ cups all-purpose flour
1 cup walnuts, ground fine
¼ cup unsweetened cocoa powder
¼ teaspoon salt
1¼ cups butter, at room temperature
¾ cup powdered sugar
1 teaspoon vodka
Powdered sugar for sprinkling

1 Preheat the oven to 325 degrees.

2 Combine the flour, walnuts, cocoa, and salt.

3 In a large bowl, cream the butter and powdered sugar. Beat in the vodka. Gradually blend in the dry ingredients.

4 Pinch off walnut-sized pieces of dough and roll into balls. Place 1½ inches apart on ungreased baking sheets.

5 Bake for 12 to 15 minutes, until lightly colored. Sprinkle with powdered sugar and transfer to wire racks to cool.

Scotch Queen Cakes

Rolled Cookies

Yield: *2 to 3 dozen*
Total time: *30 minutes*

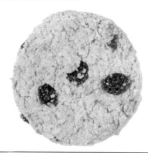

4 cups rolled oats
1 teaspoon ground cinnamon
¼ teaspoon ground nutmeg
1 cup butter, at room temperature
1 cup powdered sugar
1 cup currants

1 Preheat the oven to 350 degrees. Lightly grease 2 baking sheets.

2 Combine the oats and spices.

3 In a large bowl, cream the butter and powdered sugar. Stir in the dry ingredients. Stir in the currants. If the dough seems a little dry, add a little water ½ teaspoon at a time.

4 Divide the dough into quarters and work with one piece of dough at a time. On a floured surface, roll out each piece of dough to a 6-inch round. Place the rounds 1 inch apart on ungreased baking sheets and prick all over with a fork. Score each round into wedges.

5 Bake for 15 to 18 minutes, until lightly colored. Transfer to wire racks to cool, then cut into wedges.

Scotch Shortbread

Rolled Cookies

Yield: *2 to 3 dozen*
Total time: *30 minutes*
Chilling time: *2 hours*

2 cups (1 pound) butter, at room
   temperature
1 cup powdered sugar
4 cups all-purpose flour

1 In a large bowl, cream the butter and powdered sugar. Gradually blend in the flour to make a smooth dough. Divide the dough into quarters. Wrap in waxed paper and chill for 2 hours.

2 Preheat the oven to 350 degrees.

3 Work with one piece of dough at a time, keeping the remaining dough in the refrigerator. On a floured surface, roll out each piece of dough to a 6-inch round. Place the rounds 1 inch apart on ungreased baking sheets and prick all over with a fork. Score each round into wedges.

4 Bake for 12 to 15 minutes, until very dry and lightly colored. Transfer to wire racks to cool, then cut into wedges.

Baking notes: Be sure to use unsalted butter. This dough can also be rolled out to a thickness of ½ inch and cut into small rounds. Or it can be pressed into a 13 by-9 inch baking pan, pricked all over with a fork, and scored into bite-sized pieces.

Sesame Seed Icebox Cookies

Refrigerator Cookies

Yield: *3 to 4 dozen*
Total time: *30 minutes*
Chilling time: *8 hours*

2 cups all-purpose flour
¼ teaspoon baking soda
¼ teaspoon salt
½ cup butter, at room temperature
1 cup granulated sugar
1 large egg
¼ cup sour milk
½ cup sesame seeds, toasted

1 Combine the flour, baking soda, and salt.

2 In a large bowl, cream the butter and sugar. Beat in the egg and sour milk. Gradually blend in the dry ingredients. Stir in the sesame seeds.

3 Divide the dough in half. Form each half into a log 1 inch in diameter. Wrap in waxed paper and chill for 8 hours or overnight.

4 Preheat the oven the 375 degrees. Lightly grease 2 baking sheets.

5 Cut the logs into ¼-inch-thick slices and place 1 inch apart on the prepared baking sheets.

6 Bake for 10 to 12 minutes, until lightly colored. Transfer to wire racks to cool.

SNICKERDOODLES

Formed Cookies
YIELD: *3 to 4 dozen*
TOTAL TIME: *30 minutes*

3 cups all-purpose flour
2 teaspoons baking powder
¼ teaspoon salt
1 cup vegetable shortening
1⅓ cups granulated sugar
2 large eggs
1 teaspoon vanilla extract
3 tablespoons granulated sugar
2 teaspoons ground cinnamon

1 Preheat the oven to 350 degrees. Lightly grease 2 baking sheets.

2 Combine the flour, baking powder, and salt.

3 In a large bowl, cream the vegetable shortening and sugar. Beat in the eggs. Beat in the vanilla extract. Gradually blend in the dry ingredients.

4 In a small bowl, combine the sugar and cinnamon.

5 Pinch off 1-inch pieces of dough and roll into balls. Roll each ball in the cinnamon sugar and place 1 inch apart on the prepared baking sheets.

6 Bake for 10 to 12 minutes, until lightly colored. Transfer to wire racks to cool.

SOCKER KAKA

Drop Cookies
YIELD: *2 to 3 dozen*
TOTAL TIME: *30 minutes*

1 cup all-purpose flour
1 teaspoon baking powder
⅛ teaspoon salt
¾ cup granulated sugar
3 large eggs
1 teaspoon vanilla extract
About ¼ pint heavy cream

1 Preheat the oven to 400 degrees. Lightly grease 2 baking sheets.

2 Combine the flour, baking powder, and salt.

3 In a large bowl, beat the sugar and eggs. Beat in the vanilla extract. Gradually blend in the dry ingredients.

4 Drop by spoonfuls 2½ inches apart onto the prepared baking sheets.

5 Bake for 8 to 10 minutes, until golden brown. Immediately roll the hot cookies into cone shapes and place seam side down on wire racks to cool.

6 Whip the heavy cream until it holds soft peaks. Fill the cones with the cream and serve immediately.

Baking notes: Watch these cookies carefully; do not overbake. Chopped fruit is a nice addition to the whipped cream.

SODA CRACKER COOKIES

Bar Cookies

YIELD: *3 to 4 dozen*
TOTAL TIME: *20 minutes*

18 double-packed soda crackers
1 cup butter
1 cup packed light brown sugar
1 cup (6 ounces) semisweet choco-
    late chips
¾ cup walnuts, chopped fine

1 Preheat the oven to 375 degrees. Line a 15 by 10-inch baking pan with aluminum foil and grease it well. Line the pan with soda crackers.

2 In a medium saucepan, melt the butter. Add the brown sugar and cook, stirring until it dissolves. Bring to a boil and cook for about 3 minutes, stirring constantly. Immediately pour the mixture over the soda crackers.

3 Bake for 3 to 5 minutes, or until the mixture starts to bubble.

4 Spread the chocolate chips over the hot cookies. Let sit for a minute or so to melt the chocolate, then use a knife or spatula to spread the chocolate evenly over the top. Sprinkle with chopped walnuts. Let cool, then cut into large or small bars.

Baking notes: These are an instant favorite of everyone who tries them.

SPICE CONES

Drop Cookies

YIELD: *5 to 6 dozen*
TOTAL TIME: *30 minutes*

¾ cups all-purpose flour
1½ teaspoons ground ginger
1½ teaspoons ground nutmeg
6 tablespoons vegetable shortening
½ cup packed light brown sugar
¼ cup molasses
1 tablespoon brandy

1 Preheat the oven to 350 degrees.

2 Combine the flour and spices.

3 In a large bowl, cream the vegetable shortening and sugar. Beat in the molasses and brandy. Gradually blend in the dry ingredients.

4 Drop the dough by spoonfuls 2½ inches apart onto ungreased baking sheets.

5 Bake for 5 to 6 minutes, until golden brown. As soon as the cookies are cool enough to handle, remove them from the baking sheet and roll up around metal cone shapes. Place seam side down on wire racks to cool.

Baking notes: You will need metal cone forms for this recipe; they are available in specialty cookware shops. If the cookies harden before you are able to form them, reheat them for about 30 seconds in the oven. These cones can be filled with many types of dessert topping or ice cream. If you are filling them with ice cream, chill the cones in the freezer for at least 30 minutes before filling them. If you fill the cookies too soon, they will soften before they are served.

SPICE COOKIES

Drop Cookies

YIELD: *3 to 4 dozen*
TOTAL TIME: *30 minutes*
CHILLING TIME: *4 hours*

1 cup all-purpose flour
1 teaspoon ground cloves
½ cup vegetable shortening
1 cup granulated sugar
1 large egg
1 teaspoon vanilla extract

1 Combine the flour and cloves.

2 In a large bowl, cream the vegetable shortening and sugar. Beat in the egg. Beat in the vanilla extract. Gradually blend in the dry ingredients. Cover and chill for 4 hours.

3 Preheat the oven to 325 degrees. Lightly grease 2 baking sheets.

4 Drop the dough by spoonfuls at least 2 inches apart onto the prepared baking sheets.

5 Bake for 12 to 15 minutes, until lightly colored. Transfer to wire racks to cool.

SPRITZ COOKIES

Formed Cookies

YIELD: *3 to 4 dozen*
TOTAL TIME: *30 minutes*

2 cups all-purpose flour
⅓ cup almonds, ground fine
1 cup vegetable shortening
½ cup powdered sugar
1 large egg yolk
1 teaspoon almond extract

1 Preheat the oven to 350 degrees. Lightly grease 2 baking sheets.

2 Combine the flour and almonds.

3 In a large bowl, cream the vegetable shortening and powdered sugar. Beat in the egg yolk and almond extract. Gradually blend in the dry ingredients.

4 Place the dough in a cookie press or a pastry bag fitted with a star tip and press or pipe out into small rings onto the prepared baking sheets, spacing them 1 inch apart.

5 Bake for 8 to 10 minutes, until lightly colored. Transfer to wire racks to cool.

Baking notes: If you do not have a cookie press or pastry bag, roll out the dough on a floured surface. Using a round cutter, cut out cookies, then cut out the centers with a smaller cutter. In Sweden, where the recipe originated, the rings are traditional, but S-shaped cookies are often made from the same basic Spritz Cookie dough.

S-Shaped Cookies

Rolled Cookies

YIELD: *3 to 4 hours*
TOTAL TIME: *30 minutes*
CHILLING TIME: *4 hours*

½ cup vegetable shortening
⅔ cup granulated sugar
4 large egg yolks
½ teaspoon grated lemon zest
2 cups all-purpose flour
1 large egg white, beaten

1 In a large bowl, cream the vegetable shortening and sugar. Beat in the egg yolks. Beat in the lemon zest. Gradually blend in the flour.

2 Divide the dough into 4 pieces. Wrap in waxed paper and chill for 4 hours.

3 Preheat the oven to 350 degrees. Lightly grease 2 baking sheets.

4 Work with one piece of dough at a time, keeping the remaining dough chilled. On a floured surface, roll out the dough to a thickness of ¼ inch. Using a sharp knife, cut into strip ¾ inch wide and 4 inches long. Place the strips on the prepared baking sheets and form into the S-shapes. Brush with the beaten egg white.

5 Bake for 8 to 10 minutes, until lightly colored. Transfer to wire racks to cool.

Baking notes: Sprinkle white or colored sugar crystals over the cookies just before baking.

Sugar Cookies

Rolled Cookies

YIELD: *3 to 4 dozen*
TOTAL TIME: *40 minutes*

3 cups all-purpose flour
2 teaspoons baking powder
½ teaspoon baking soda
½ teaspoon salt
⅔ cup butter, at room temperature
1 cup granulated sugar
2 large eggs
¼ cup buttermilk
½ teaspoon brandy
Milk for glazing
Granulated sugar for sprinkling

1 Preheat the oven to 375 degrees. Lightly grease 2 baking sheets.

2 Combine the flour, baking powder, baking soda, and salt.

3 In a large bowl, cream the butter and sugar. Beat in the eggs. Beat in the buttermilk and brandy. Gradually blend in the dry ingredients.

4 On a floured surface, roll out the dough to a thickness of ¼ inch. Using a 2-inch round cookie cutter, cut out cookies and place 1½ inches apart on the prepared baking sheets. Brush with milk and sprinkle liberally with granulated sugar.

5 Bake for 10 to 12 minutes, until lightly colored. Transfer to wire racks to cool.

THIMBLES

Formed Cookies
YIELD: *3 to 4 dozen*
TOTAL TIME: *30 minutes*

1 cup vegetable shortening
½ cup packed light brown sugar
2 large eggs, separated
1½ teaspoons vanilla extract
2¼ cups all-purpose flour
1½ cups almonds, ground
About ¼ cup fruit preserves

1 Preheat the oven to 350 degrees. Lightly grease 2 baking sheets.

2 In a large bowl, cream the vegetable shortening and brown sugar. Beat in the egg yolks and vanilla extract. Gradually blend in the flour.

3 In a small bowl, beat the egg whites stiff until stiff but not dry.

4 Pinch off small pieces of dough and roll into balls. Roll the balls in the beaten egg white, then in the ground almonds, and place 1 inch apart on the prepared baking sheets. With your finger, press an indentation into the center of each ball.

5 Bake for 12 to 15 minutes, until lightly colored. Fill each cookie with a dab of fruit preserves, then transfer to wire racks to cool.

Baking notes: These are good filled with preserves; but for a real treat, fill them with a lemon custard or banana custard. Even Jell-O can be used: Chill the cookies, then spoon the Jell-O into the cookies just before it sets.

TOSCA COOKIES

Drop Cookies
YIELD: *3 to 4 dozen*
TOTAL TIME: *30 minutes*
CHILLING TIME: *2 hours*

1 cup all-purpose flour
⅓ cup almonds, ground
⅓ cup farina ceral, such as Cream of Wheat
½ teaspoon baking powder
1 cup vegetable shortening
⅔ cup granulated sugar
1 large egg

GLAZE
4 tablespoons butter, melted
6 tablespoons granulated sugar
1 teaspoon corn syrup
⅓ cup slivered almonds

1 Combine the flour, almonds, farina, and baking powder.

2 In a large bowl, cream the vegetable shortening and sugar. Beat in the egg. Gradually blend in the dry ingredients. Cover and chill for 2 hours.

3 Preheat the oven to 350 degrees. Lightly grease 2 baking sheets.

4 To make the glaze, combine the butter, sugar, and corn syrup in a small bowl and beat until smooth.

5 Drop the dough by spoonfuls 1½ inches apart onto the prepared baking sheets.

6 Bake for 10 to 12 minutes, just until lightly colored. Brush the cookies with the glaze, sprinkle with the slivered almonds, and bake for 5 minutes longer. Transfer to wire racks to cool.

TRAIL MIX COOKIES

Drop Cookies

YIELD: *3 to 4 dozen*
TOTAL TIME: *30 minutes*

¾ cup all-purpose flour
½ teaspoon baking soda
½ cup vegetable shortening
1 cup packed light brown sugar
½ cup peanut butter
1 large egg
1 teaspoon vanilla extract
1 cup (6 ounces) semisweet chocolate chips
1 cup raisins
⅔ cup peanuts, chopped

1 Preheat the oven to 375 degrees. Lightly grease 2 baking sheets.

2 Combine the flour and baking soda.

3 In a large bowl, cream the vegetable shortening and brown-sugar. Beat in the peanut butter.

Beat in the egg and vanilla extract. Gradually blend in the dry ingredients. Fold in the chocolate chips, raisins, and peanuts.

4 Drop the dough by spoonfuls 1½ inches apart onto the prepared baking sheets.

5 Bake for 10 to 12 minutes, until lightly colored. Transfer to wire racks to cool.

6 When the cookies are cool, wrap individually and store in an airtight container.

UPPÅKRA COOKIES

Rolled Cookies

YIELD: *4 to 6 dozen*
TOTAL TIME: *35 minutes*

3½ cups all-purpose flour
2 cups potato flour (see Baking notes)
1¾ cups butter, at room temperature
1 cup granulated sugar
2 large eggs, beaten
Powdered sugar for sprinkling
About 1 cup whole almonds

1 Preheat the oven to 425 degrees. Lightly grease 2 baking sheets.

2 Combine the two flours.

3 In a large bowl, cream the butter and sugar. Gradually blend in the flour.

4 On a floured surface, roll out the dough to a thickness of ⅛ inch. Using a 1½-inch round cookie cutter, cut out cookies and place 1 inch apart on the prepared baking sheets. Brush with the beaten eggs and sprinkle with powdered sugar. Push a whole almond into the center of each cookie.

5 Bake for 8 to 10 minutes, until lightly colored. Transfer to wire racks to cool.

Baking notes: Potato flour can be found at specialty food stores. You can also use 1 cup of potato starch in place of the potato flour and increase the all-purpose flour to 4½ cups.

Vanilla Daisies

Rolled Cookies
YIELD: *3 to 4 dozen*
TOTAL TIME: *30 minutes*

2⅓ cups all-purpose flour
½ teaspoon baking powder
¼ teaspoon salt
1 cup vegetable shortening
⅔ cup granulated sugar
1 large egg
1 teaspoon vanilla extract
1 teaspoon grated lemon zest
About ¼ cup glacé cherries, cut in
   half

1 Preheat the oven to 350
degrees.

2 Combine the flour, baking
powder, and salt.

3 In a large bowl, cream the vegetable shortening and sugar. Beat
in the egg and vanilla extract.
Beat in the lemon zest. Gradually
blend in the dry ingredients.

4 On a floured surface, roll the
dough out to a thickness of ¼
inch. Using a flower-shaped
cookie cutter, cut out cookies and
place 1 inch apart on ungreased
baking sheets. Press a half-cherry
into the center of each cookie.

5 Bake for 10 to 12 minutes, until
lightly colored. Transfer to wire
racks to cool.

Vanilla Hearts

Rolled Cookies
YIELD: *3 to 6 dozen*
TOTAL TIME: *30 minutes*
CHILLING TIME: *2 hours*

4 cups all-purpose flour
½ teaspoon salt
⅔ cup vegetable shortening
1 cup granulated sugar
3 large eggs
1 teaspoon vanilla extract

1 Combine the flour and salt.

2 In a large bowl, cream the vegetable shortening and sugar. Beat
in the eggs one at a time. Beat in
the vanilla extract. Gradually
blend in the dry ingredients.
Cover and chill for at least 2
hours.

3 Preheat the oven to 350
degrees. Lightly grease 2 baking
sheets.

4 On a floured surface, roll out
the dough to a thickness of ¼
inch. Using a heart-shaped
cookie cutter, cut out cookies and
place 1 inch apart on the prepared baking sheets.

5 Bake for 10 to 12 minutes, until
lightly colored. Transfer to wire
racks to cool.

Baking notes: Decorate these
cookies with white or pink icing.

Vanilla Sour Cream Rosettes

Formed Cookies

YIELD: *3 to 4 dozen*
TOTAL TIME: *30 minutes*

1½ cups all-purpose flour
½ teaspoon baking powder
⅛ teaspoon baking soda
¼ teaspoon salt
¼ cup butter, at room temperature
½ cup granulated sugar
1 large egg
¼ cup sour cream
1 teaspoon vanilla extract

1 Preheat the oven to 350 degrees.

2 Combine the flour, baking powder, baking soda, and salt.

3 In a large bowl, cream the butter and sugar. Beat in the egg. Beat in the sour cream. Beat in the vanilla extract. Gradually blend in the dry ingredients.

4 Place the dough in a cookie press or a pastry bag fitted with a star tip and press or pipe out small rosettes 1 inch apart onto ungreased baking sheets.

5 Bake for 10 to 12 minutes, until lightly colored. Transfer to wire racks to cool.

Vanilla Sugar Cookies

Rolled Cookies

YIELD: *3 to 5 dozen*
TOTAL TIME: *30 minutes*
CHILLING TIME: *1 hour*

2½ cups all-purpose flour
1 teaspoon baking powder
Pinch of salt
1 cup butter, at room temperature
1 cup granulated sugar
2 large egg yolks
1½ teaspoons vanilla extract
Granulated sugar for sprinkling

1 Combine the flour, baking powder, and salt.

2 In a large bowl, cream the butter and sugar. Beat in the egg yolks. Beat in the vanilla extract. Gradually blend in the dry ingredients. Cover and chill for 1 hour.

3 Preheat the oven to 375 degrees. Lightly grease 2 baking sheets.

4 On a floured surface, roll out the dough to a thickness of ¼ inch. Using a 2-inch round cookie cutter, cut out cookies and place 1 inch apart onto the prepared baking sheets.

5 Bake for 10 to 12 minutes, until lightly colored. Sprinkle granulated sugar over the hot cookies and transfer to wire racks to cool.

VICEROYS

Drop Cookies
YIELD: *4 to 6 dozen*
TOTAL TIME: *30 minutes*

3 cups all-purpose flour
1 cup pecans, ground fine
1½ teaspoons baking powder
1½ cups vegetable shortening
1½ cups granulated sugar
2 large eggs
2 teaspoons Tía Maria liqueur
⅓ cup warm water

1 Preheat the oven to 350 degrees. Lightly grease 2 baking sheets.

2 Combine the flour, pecans, and baking powder.

3 In a large bowl, cream the vegetable shortening and sugar. Beat in the eggs one at a time. Beat in the Tía Maria and water. Gradually blend in the dry ingredients.

4 Drop the dough by spoonfuls 1½ inches apart onto the prepared baking sheets.

5 Bake for 12 to 15 minutes, until lightly colored. Transfer to wire racks to cool.

VIENNESE CRESCENTS

Formed Cookies
YIELD: *4 to 5 dozen*
TOTAL TIME: *45 minutes*

2 cups all-purpose flour
1 cup hazelnuts, ground fine
1 cup vegetable shortening
½ cup granulated sugar
1 teaspoon Gilka liqueur (see Baking notes)
Powdered sugar for rolling

1 Preheat the oven to 325 degrees.

2 Combine the flour and hazelnuts.

3 In a large bowl, cream the vegetable shortening and sugar. Beat in the Gilka. Gradually blend in the dry ingredients.

4 Pinch off pieces of dough, form into crescents, and place the crescents 1½ inches apart on ungreased baking sheets.

5 Bake for 25 to 30 minutes, until lightly colored. Roll the crescents in powdered sugar and transfer to wire racks to cool, then roll in powdered sugar a second time.

Baking notes: Gilka is a nearly colorless liqueur, highly spiced with caraway seed; Kummel could be substituted.

VIRGINIA REBELS

Drop Cookies

YIELD: *3 to 4 dozen*
TOTAL TIME: *30 minutes*

1 cup all-purpose flour
6 tablespoons unsweetened cocoa
  powder
½ teaspoon baking soda
½ teaspoon salt
1¼ cups vegetable shortening
1½ cups granulated sugar
1 large egg
¼ cup water
½ teaspoon whiskey
3 cups rolled oats

1 Preheat the oven to 350 degrees.

2 Combine the flour, cocoa powder, baking soda, and salt.

3 In a large bowl, cream the vegetable shortening and sugar. Beat in the egg. Beat in the water and whiskey. Gradually blend in the dry ingredients. Stir in the oats.

4 Drop the dough by spoonfuls 1½ inches apart onto ungreased baking sheets.

5 Bake for 10 to 12 minutes, or until lightly colored. Transfer to wire racks to cool.

WALNUT SHORTBREAD

Formed Cookies

YIELD: *4 to 5 dozen*
TOTAL TIME: *30 minutes*

4½ cups all-purpose flour
1 cup walnuts, ground fine
2 cups vegetable shortening
2½ cups packed light brown sugar
2 teaspoons vanilla extract

1 Preheat the oven to 350 degrees.

2 Combine the flour and walnuts.

3 In a large bowl, cream the vegetable shortening and brown sugar. Beat in the vanilla extract. Gradually blend in the dry ingredients.

4 Pinch off walnut-sized pieces of dough and roll into balls. Place 1½ inches apart on ungreased baking sheets. Flatten with the back of a spoon dipped in flour.

5 Bake for 10 to 15 minutes, until lightly colored. Transfer to wire racks to cool.

Wheat Flake Jumbles

Drop Cookies

Yield: *3 to 4 dozen*
Total time: *30 minutes*

1 cup all-purpose flour
½ teaspoon baking powder
¼ teaspoon baking soda
¼ teaspoon salt
⅓ cup vegetable shortening
½ cup packed light brown sugar
1 large egg
1½ tablespoons sour milk
1 teaspoon vanilla extract
½ cup dates, pitted and chopped
    fine
½ cup walnuts, chopped
1½ cups cornflakes

1 Preheat the oven to 375 degrees. Lightly grease 2 baking sheets.

2 Combine the flour, baking powder, baking soda, and salt.

3 In a large bowl, cream the vegetable shortening and brown sugar. Beat in the egg. Beat in the sour milk and vanilla extract. Gradually blend in the dry ingredients. Fold in the dates and walnuts.

4 Spread the cornflakes in a pie plate.

5 Drop the dough by spoonfuls onto the cornflakes and roll in the cornflakes until completely coated. Place 3 inches apart on the prepared baking sheets.

6 Bake for 12 to 15 minutes, until golden brown. Transfer to wire racks to cool.

Whole Wheat Cookies

Drop Cookies

Yield: *4 to 6 dozen*
Total time: *30 minutes*
Chilling time: *2 hours*

1 cup all-purpose flour
1 cup whole wheat flour
2 teaspoons baking powder
¼ teaspoon baking soda
¼ teaspoon salt
1 cup vegetable shortening
¾ cup granulated sugar
1 large egg
1 cup mashed, cooked carrots
1 teaspoon lemon extract
½ teaspoon vanilla extract
1 cup walnuts, chopped (optional)
1 cup raisins (optional)

1 Combine the two flours, the baking powder, baking soda, and salt.

2 In a large bowl, cream the vegetable shortening and sugar. Beat in the egg. Beat in the carrots. Beat in the lemon extract and vanilla extract. Gradually blend in the dry ingredients. Fold in the optional walnuts and raisins. Cover and chill for 2 hours.

3 Preheat the oven to 375 degrees. Lightly grease 2 baking sheets.

4 Drop the dough by spoonfuls 1½ inches apart onto the prepared baking sheets.

5 Bake for 10 to 12 minutes, until lightly colored. Transfer to wire racks to cool.

WHOOPIE PIES

Drop Cookies

YIELD: *3 to 4 dozen*
TOTAL TIME: *30 minutes*

2 cups all-purpose flour
6 tablespoons carob powder
2 teaspoons baking powder
½ teaspoon salt
⅓ cup vegetable shortening
1 cup powdered sugar
1 large egg
1 cup skim milk
1 teaspoon crème de cacao
½ cup white chocolate chips

FILLING
¾ cup vegetable shortening
1 cup powdered sugar
1 teaspoon coffee liqueur
½ cup store-bought marshmallow
   topping

1 Preheat the oven to 375 degrees. Lightly grease 2 baking sheets.

2 Combine the flour, carob powder, baking powder, and salt.

3 In a large bowl, cream the vegetable shortening and powdered sugar. Beat in the egg. Beat in the milk and crème de cacao. Gradually blend in the dry ingredients. Fold in the chocolate chips.

4 Drop the dough by heaping tablespoonfuls 3 inches apart onto the prepared baking sheets.

5 Bake for 7 to 10 minutes, until a toothpick inserted in the center comes out clean. Transfer to wire racks to cool.

6 To make the filling, beat the vegetable shortening and powdered sugar in a medium bowl. Beat in the coffee liqueur. Beat in the marshmallow topping.

7 To assemble, cut the cookies horizontally in half. Spread the filling liberally over the bottoms and sandwich with the tops.

Baking notes: To make more uniform cookies, you can use crumpet or muffin rings to form the pies.

Zwieback

Formed Cookies

YIELD: *2 to 3 dozen*
TOTAL TIME: *50 minutes*

1½ cups all-purpose flour
½ cup almonds, ground
1½ teaspoons baking powder
½ cup vegetable shortening
½ cup granulated sugar
2 large eggs
2 teaspoons amaretto

1 Preheat the oven to 325 degrees.

2 Combine the flour, almonds, and baking powder.

3 In a large bowl, cream the vegetable shortening and sugar. Beat in the eggs one at a time. Beat in amaretto. Gradually blend in the dry ingredients.

4 Shape the dough into a loaf 13 inches long and 2½ inches wide and place on an ungreased baking sheet.

5 Bake for 18 minutes, or until firm to the touch.

6 Transfer the loaf to a cutting boards and cut into ½-inch-thick slices. Cut each slice in half diagonally. Place the slices on the baking sheets and bake for 20 minutes. Turn off the oven and leave the cookies in the oven 20 minutes longer; do not open the oven door. Transfer to wire racks to cool.

INGREDIENTS

NUTS

Most nuts are available in a variety of forms, including unshelled or shelled, blanched (peeled or skinned) or unblanched, chopped, halved, sliced, or slivered. Cashew nuts are unique in that they are not sold in the shell. Although walnuts, almonds, and pecans are the nuts most commonly used in baking, many other types can result in delicious cookies and baked goods—hazelnuts and hickory nuts, to name just two.

The most inexpensive way to purchase any nuts is in the shell. As a general rule of thumb, one pound of unshelled nuts will equal half a pound of shelled. However, for ease and convenience, many home bakers prefer to buy shelled nuts. Although nuts in the shell stay fresh for a long time, keeping them in the lower part of the refrigerator will prolong their shelf life. Shelled nuts turn rancid quickly and are best kept in airtight containers in the freezer.

The recipes in this book use sliced, slivered, chopped, and ground nuts as well as whole nuts. Chopped means that the nuts are in small corn kernel-size chunks. Ground is when the nut has been reduced to a very coarse, almost powder form.

Almond The fruit of the almond tree can be purchased shelled or unshelled, blanched, or unblanched, slivered, sliced, and chopped. The shell is soft and easy to crack open. Unblanched almonds have a soft brown color; blanched nuts are a pale ivory color.

Black Walnuts Black walnuts were once used extensively in baking recipes, but more widely available English walnuts have replaced them in popularity. Black Walnuts are still preferred by many cooks and bakers; if you come across them, you will want to try baking with these flavorful nuts.

Brazil Nut Although brazil nuts were once available only during the Christmas holiday season, now they are available all year long. They are large nuts most effectively used ground or chopped in cookie recipes.

Cashew This is one of the most popular eating nuts in the world. For baking purposes they are considered a soft nut.

Chestnuts Chestnuts are available fresh in the winter and canned all year around. The best way to prepare fresh chestnuts for cookie recipes is to score them on the bottom and toast them in the oven to loosen their outer shells and skins.

English Walnuts In the United States this is the most

popular nut for cooking purposes. (See Black Walnuts.)

Filbert (See Hazelnuts.)

Hazelnuts The hazelnut, also called filbert, is one of the most flavorful of all nuts. Hazelnuts are far more popular in Europe than in the United States, which is unfortunate in light of the nut's rich taste.

Macadamia Nuts The macadamia nut is one of the most expensive nuts in the world, partly, no doubt, because it takes up to five years before the macadamia tree can start to bear fruit. In addition, macadamia nut trees have never been successfully transplanted to mainland United States. Macadamia nuts have a rich, buttery flavor and are usually toasted in coconut oil.

Peanut This small slick nut (actually a legume), is the most popular eating nut in the United States. Half of the peanut crop is blended into peanut butter, but peanuts turn up in a variety of baked goods, including peanut butter cookies, a perennial favorite.

Pecans Many cooks and bakers prefer the pecan to any other nut; pecans are especially popular in the southern regions of the United States, where they grow profusely.

Pine Nuts Known as *piñon* in Spanish and *pignola* in Italian, the pine nut is usually considered more of an eating nut

than a baking nut, but it works very well in a variety of cookies because of its rich, full flavor.

Pistachio Nuts These nuts, when shelled and toasted work extremely well in cookies because of their complex flavor that melds so well with a variety of spices.

FRUITS

Hundreds of cookie recipes that include fruit in various states—fresh, dried, or frozen.

Dried fruit should be rehydrated before use. The process of rehydration is simply nothing more than soaking the dried fruit in boiling water or another liquid.

Apples Although apples are available throughout the year, they are at their peak in the fall. Cored and sliced dried apples should usually be hydrated before they are used. Applesauce is added to many recipes both to make the cookies softer and to give them a fresh apple taste. Canned apples are not suitable for cookies.

Apricots Fresh apricots are generally available only in season, from May through July. But dried apricots are delicious. Canned apricots tend to be flavorless if used for baking.

Bananas Bananas are available every day of the year. There are two varieties: One is for eating and drying, the other, easily recognizable by its dark skin color, is for cooking. The cooking banana is also smaller than the eating banana. Most home bakers use the eating variety for cooking. Dried banana chips are also available.

Berries Fresh berries including strawberries, blackberries, blueberries, boysenberries, raspberries, black raspberries, are available only in season. We are fortunate that they are always available in the form of jams and preserves which are used in many cookie recipes.

Cherries Fresh cherries are seldom used in cookie baking. They are seldom used as an additive in cookies. (See Glacé/Candied Cherries.)

Dates The fruit of the date palm tree has been used for centuries, as far back as ancient Egypt, as a means of sweetening dishes. Most of the recipes here call for pitted dates.

Figs It is surprising that so few cookie recipes use figs. Fig Newtons are one of this country's most popular cookies.

Lemon Zest Zest and juice of the lemon rind is seldom used in any state other than grated. This adds a pleasing lemon flavor to the cookies in which it is used.

Orange Zest Only the zest and the juice of the orange may be used in baking. The cookies using this zest may have a subtle or strong flavor,

depending upon the amounts used.

Peaches Only dried peaches are appropriate for cookies; canned peaches do not hold up under the heat of cooking and become mushy. Fresh peaches may be sliced and layered in bar cookies. Peach puree can be used as a flavor in cookie recipes.

Persimmons A seasonal fruit with a sweet flavor, the persimmon really isn't edible until it is overripe. When the skin starts to turn brown and the pulp inside becomes almost mushy, it is ready to eat or use.

Pineapple Pineapples are readily available all year round, but for baking the canned fruit is most popular because of ease of preparation. It should be well drained before using. Candied pineapple is also good in cookies.

Prunes Dried prunes are used pitted, sliced, or diced in recipes.

SPICES AND HERBS

Allspice These berries, the seeds of the allspice tree, are harvested and sun-dried until they are a deep reddish brown. They are made available whole and ground. Their flavor resembles a soft blend of cloves, cinnamon, and nutmeg (hence the name). Allspice is used to flavor cakes, pies, cookies, and breads. It is especially good in pastries made with fruit.

Anise Anise seeds, or aniseed, are greenish brown with a strong licorice flavor. They are available whole or crushed. Anise seeds are used extensively in cookies and fruit pies, especially in holiday specialties.

Apple pie spice This is a commercial blend of cinnamon, cloves, nutmeg, and some other sweet-type spices. It is used mainly for pies, but in baking, it can be substituted in any recipe that calls for cinnamon or nutmeg.

Caraway seeds Small greenish brown crescent-shaped seeds. Although caraway seeds are perhaps most associated with rye bread, they can be very flavorful in cookies and cakes. The seeds are always sold whole.

Cardamom A member of the ginger family, has a long history; its use has been documented as early as the fourth century B.C. It is available whole or ground. Its sweet flavor makes it a favorite spice in Danish pastries, and it is also used in cakes of all kinds and many cookies. Cardamom is the third most expensive spice in the world.

Cinnamon The bark of a laurel tree; it and its cousin cassia are the two oldest spices known. Both are available in reddish brown rolled sticks or ground. Its sweet pungent taste makes cinnamon one of our most popular spices, used in cakes, pies, cookies, breads, puddings, and other baked goods.

Cloves Cloves are the dried bud of a tropical tree. They have a strong, pungent flavor. Cloves are available both whole and ground; the ground form is used in many cakes, cookies, pies, and fruit desserts; whole cloves are occasionally used in sweets, such as baklava.

Coriander The seed of the coriander, or cilantro plant; it is available whole or ground. The ground seeds are used in cookies, cakes, pies, candies, and other sweets.

Cumin An aromatic seed very similar to caraway seeds in flavor. It is available as seeds or ground.

English spice Commercial blend of several spices with a predominately cinnamon-allspice flavor. It can be used on its own or as a substitute in any baked good that calls for cinnamon, allspice, nutmeg, and cloves.

Fennel seeds These have a mild licorice flavor. They are used in breads and breakfast baked goods.

Ginger Fresh ginger, or ginger root, and the powdered, or dried spice have a hot sweet-spicy flavor. Ginger, both fresh and dried, is used in cakes, breads, cookies, and fruit desserts. Crystallized, or candied, ginger is preserved fresh ginger that has been rolled in sugar.

Mace The lacy outer membrane-like covering of the shell of the nutmeg. Its flavor is sweet, warm, and highly spicy. Mace is usually seen as a powder, but it is also available in flakes or blades.

Mint A perennial herb; peppermint and spearmint are the most popular varieties for flavorings. The dried leaves are available whole, crushed, and powdered.

Nutmeg The seed of the nutmeg tree. It has a sweet-hot taste and a pungent aroma. Available whole or ground, it is used in cakes, pies and cookies. (See Mace.)

Poppy seeds These have a sweet nut-like taste. The tiny black seeds are used extensively to garnish breads, rolls, and cookies.

Sesame seeds Known as benne seeds in the South, these are used to garnish breads, rolls, and cookies. When toasted, the seeds have a very nutty flavor.

Vanilla bean The seed capsule of the vanilla orchid. From this bean is derived the flavoring used to make vanilla extract. The bean itself is used in the preparation of vanilla sugar.

Vanilla extract A liquid derived from the vanilla bean and used extensively as a flavoring in baking and cooking. Synthetic vanillas are available for a lesser price.

CHOCOLATE

For our purposes, cocoa powder, unsweetened chocolate, semisweet or bittersweet chocolate, chocolate syrup, and chocolate chips are the foundations of the world of the chocolate cookie.

Unsweetened chocolate means baker's-style chocolate. Baker's-style chocolate is bitter chocolate and is the base for most other chocolate products. It can be found in the supermarket in the baking section in 14- to 16-ounce packages. The chocolate is divided into small squares, and each square weighs one ounce.

Semisweet chocolate, sometimes called bittersweet, is packaged the same way, too, but there is a wide variety of imported bittersweet or semisweet chocolate available as well.

Cocoa is the powdered form of chocolate. For baking, use unsweetened cocoa powder, not the sweet cocoa for drinking.

Milk chocolate has long been a favorite of the candy-loving public. But milk chocolate can't be used interchangeably with other types of chocolate in most recipes.

White chocolate has gained in popularity in recent years. White chocolate is not actually chocolate, because it contains no chocolate liquor. It is cocoa butter with sugar and milk added.

Many of the recipes in this book call for melting chocolate. It isn't difficult if you follow a few separate rules. Chocolate should always be melted over low heat in an absolutely dry pan. *Dry* is the key word. When you are melting chocolate by itself, the slightest drop of liquid or moisture can cause the chocolate to seize, or to become stiff and lumpy. (If you are adding other ingredients, the general rule of thumb is one tablespoon of liquid to one ounce of chocolate. It is the minute amounts of liquid that cause the trouble.) *For this reason, the pan melting the chocolate in should never be covered* because condensation may form on the lid and drip into the chocolate. If chocolate should seize, you often can save it by stirring in one teaspoon per ounce of chocolate of vegetable shortening. (*Do not use butter or margarine.*)

Chocolate burns easily, so using a double boiler is recommended. If you don't have one, you can put the chocolate in a heatproof cup and place it in a saucepan partially filled with water, over very low heat. (Milk chocolate should be melted at a lower temperature than unsweetened or semisweet chocolate.) Then stir the chocolate occasionally, until it is smooth.

A microwave oven also works well for melting. Consult your owner's manual for instructions with your particular microwave.

MISCELLANEOUS

Candied Beads *(Silver or Gold Balls)* Candied beads or balls have been around for many years. They are used more for decoration, especially for holiday cookies.

Candied Citron The citron is rarely available in the United States. At a time when oranges and lemons were not readily available, its peel was used in place of other members of the citrus family.

Chocolate Candies Usually the chocolate candies used in cookies are of the wafer type, such as mints or pralines.

Chocolate Chips In the early 1900s Ruth Wakefield, who worked at the The Tollhouse Inn in Massachusetts, chopped a baker's style bar of chocolate and added the pieces to a batch of cookie dough, making the first chocolate chip cookies. Because of that woman's inventiveness, a whole industry developed. In addition to semisweet chocolate chips, there are now butterscotch, peanut butter, and white chocolate used in baking.

Glacé/Candied Cherries This form of dried cherries sweetened with sugar are used diced up in cookie recipes, and as decorative toppings on cookies.

Jelly Candies Like other candies, they are used more for a decoration than for flavor. Jelly candies and gumdrops are used whole, or are chopped and added to the dough.

Jimmies These candies come in chocolate or rainbow colors, and are a great addition to many cookies.

Sugar Crystals These are sprinkled on the cookies after they have been formed and or baked. Like candy beads, they are added to a cookie strictly for decoration. They come colored or white.

FLAVORINGS

Using liqueur or brandy in cookie recipes opens up a whole new world of flavoring possibilities, while keeping your costs at a minimum.

Each liqueur or brandy listed below is as economical as a small 1- or 2-ounce bottle of vanilla extract. If the products are kept well-corked or capped, there is little chance of them going bad before you have time to use them. Also, most of the imitation flavoring products have little or no alcohol, and have a better chance of going bad than the flavored liqueur. There is a world of flavoring out there in addition to those you see in the grocery store.

ALTERNATIVE FLAVORINGS

Liqueur/Brandy	*Flavor*
Abisante	anise and herb
Advokaat	eggnog
Ari	plum
Amaretto	apricot almond
Amaretto/Cognac	amaretto
Ambrosia Liqueur	caramel
Amer Picon	orange
Anisette	anise
Antioqueno	anise
Apry	apricot
Arak	rum
Ashanti Gold	chocolate
Averna Liqueur	herbal
Irish Cream	fresh cream
Baitz Island Creme	almond
	coconut
	chocolate
Barenjäger	honey
Benedictine	herbal
Blackberry Brandy	blackberry
Boggs Cranberry	cranberry
Bucca di Amore	anise
	herb
	spices
Cafe Brizard	coffee
Cafe orange	coffee & orange
Cafe Lolita	coffee
Campari	orange/caramel
	vanilla
Carmella	vanilla
Chambord Liqueur	raspberry
	fruit
	herb
	honey
CherriStock	cherry
Cherry Brandy	cherry

Liqueur/Brandy	Flavor
Choclair	chocolate/coconut
Cinnamon Schnapps	cinnamon
Club Raki	licorice
Coffee Brandy	coffee
Coffee Liqueur	coffee
Cranberria	cranberry
Conticream	chocolate cream
Crème de Almond	almond
Crème de Banana	banana
Crème de Cacao	chocolate
Crème de Cafe	coffee
Crème de Cassis	black currant
Crème de Framboise	raspberry
Crème de Menthe	peppermint
Crème de Prunella	plum
Crème de Strawberry	strawberry
Cuarenta Y Tres	vanilla
Droste Bittersweet	bittersweet chocolate
Fraise des Bois	wild strawberry
Ginger Brandy	ginger
Ginger Schnapps	ginger
Kümmel	caraway
Lemonier	lemon
Lemonique	tart lemon
Mandarinette	tangerines
Mandarino	tangy orange
	cherry
Marron Liqueur	chestnut
Midori	honeydew melon
Paso Fino Rum	rum
Peach Brandy	peach
Pear William	Anjou pear
Peppermint Schnapps	peppermint
Peter Herring	cherry
Praline Liqueur	vanilla & pecan
Spearmint Schnapps	spearmint
Straretto	strawberry

PANTRY

These recipes are standard frostings, icings, fillings, and bar cookie crusts. They are referenced for use throughout the main cookie recipe text.

FROSTINGS AND ICINGS

RICH BUTTERCREAM
YIELD: 2 TO 2½ CUPS
½ cup butter, at room temperature
3½ cups powdered sugar
⅛ teaspoon salt
1 large egg yolk
About 1 tablespoon milk

In a large bowl, cream the butter. Beat in the powdered sugar. Beat in the salt and egg yolk. Add just enough milk to make a spreadable frosting. Flavor the buttercream with any of the following suggestions, or add a flavoring of your own choice. (Note: Buttercream frostings have a tendency to soften during hot weather. If this happens, beat in a little cornstarch to bring the mixture back to the desired consistency.)

For the following flavored buttercreams use the Rich Buttercream recipe with the added flavorings.

VANILLA BUTTERCREAM
Add 1 teaspoon vanilla extract.

ALMOND BUTTERCREAM
Add 1 teaspoon almond extract or Amaretto.

ORANGE BUTTERCREAM
Add 1 teaspoon orange liqueur.

LEMON BUTTERCREAM
Add 1 teaspoon lemon extract.

RUM BUTTERCREAM
Add 1 teaspoon rum.

BRANDY BUTTERCREAM
Add 1 teaspoon brandy or cognac.

COCOA BUTTERCREAM
Add 1 teaspoon crème de cacao.

RASPBERRY BUTTERCREAM
Add 1 teaspoon raspberry liqueur.

COFFEE BUTTERCREAM
Add 1 teaspoon strong coffee.

APRICOT BUTTERCREAM
Add 1 teaspoon apricot brandy.

DECORATING BUTTERCREAM
YIELD: 4 TO 4½ CUPS
2 cups vegetable shortening
4 cups powdered sugar
1 to 2 large egg whites
Pinch of salt
Vanilla or other flavoring to taste

In a large bowl, cream the shortening. Gradually beat in the powdered sugar. Beat in the egg whites. Beat in the salt. Beat in the flavoring. Remember that a little flavoring goes a long way; think in terms of drops, not spoonfuls. (Note: Buttercream frostings have a tendency to soften during hot weather. If this happens, beat in a little cornstarch to bring the mixture back to the desired consistency.)

CHOCOLATE FROSTING I
YIELD: 2 TO 2½ CUPS
5⅓ tablespoon butter, at room temperature
½ cup Dutch process unsweetened cocoa powder
Pinch of salt
3 tablespoons boiling water
1½ cups powdered sugar, or more if necessary

In a large bowl, cream the butter. Beat in the cocoa. Add the salt and boiling water, stirring until you have a smooth paste. Beat in the powdered sugar and beat until the frosting reaches a spreadable consistency. If it seems too thick, add a few drops of water; if it seems too thin, add a little more powdered sugar.

CHOCOLATE FROSTING II

YIELD: 1 TO 1½ CUPS

1½ ounces unsweetened chocolate, chopped

1 tablespoon butter, at room temperature

¼ cup sour cream

½ teaspoon vanilla extract

1½ cups powdered sugar, or more if necessary

Melt the chocolate in a double boiler over low heat, stirring until smooth. Remove from the heat and beat in the butter and sour cream. Beat in the vanilla extract. Gradually beat in the powdered sugar and beat until the frosting reaches a spreadable consistency. If it seems too thick, add a few drops of water; if it seems too thin, add a little more powdered sugar.

CHOCOLATE FROSTING III

YIELD: 1 TO 1¼ CUPS

1 cup (6 ounces) semisweet chocolate chips

2 teaspoons boiling water

2 tablespoons light corn syrup

2 teaspoons strong brewed coffee

Place the chocolate chips in a small bowl and pour the boiling water over them. Start beating and add the corn syrup and coffee. If it seems too thick, add a few drops of water; if it seems too thin, add a little more powdered sugar.

DARK CHOCOLATE ICING

YIELD: 1 TO 1½ CUPS

6 ounces unsweetened chocolate, chopped

2 tablespoons butter, at room temperature

1 teaspoon vanilla extract

⅛ teaspoon salt

2 cups powdered sugar

⅓ cup milk

Melt the chocolate in the top of a double boiler over low heat, stirring until smooth. Remove from the heat and beat in the butter. Beat in the vanilla and salt. Gradually beat in the powdered sugar. Beat in just enough milk to make a spreadable frosting.

VANILLA ICING I

YIELD: ABOUT ½ CUP

½ cup powdered sugar

1 tablespoon water

Put the powdered sugar in a small bowl. Beat in the water and continue beating until the icing reaches the desired consistency. If the icing is too thick, add more water; if it is too thin, add more powdered sugar.

VANILLA ICING II

YIELD: 2 TO 2¼ CUPS

3 cups powdered sugar

⅓ cup evaporated milk

1½ teaspoons vanilla extract

Put 1 cup of the powdered sugar in a medium bowl and beat in the milk and vanilla extract. Gradually beat in the remaining 2 cups powdered sugar and continue beating until the icing reaches the desired consistency. If the icing is too thick, add more water; if it is too thin, add more powdered sugar.

GREEN CRÈME DE MENTHE ICING

YIELD: 2 TO 2¼ CUPS

Use the same ingredients as in Vanilla Icing II, except replace the vanilla extract with 1½ teaspoons green crème de menthe liqueur, and follow the same instructions.

LEMON SUGAR ICING

YIELD: ABOUT ½ CUP

½ cup powdered sugar

1 teaspoon fresh lemon juice

1 tablespoon water

Put the powdered sugar in a small bowl. Beat in the lemon

juice and water and continue beating until the icing reaches the desired consistency. If the icing is too thick add more water; if it is too thin add more powdered sugar.

Baking notes: For a tarter lemon taste, use lemon extract in place if the lemon juice.

ALMOND CREAM FILLING

YIELD: 1¾ TO 2 CUPS

Combine 1½ cups heavy cream, 1 cup powdered sugar, and 1 cup finely ground almonds in a medium saucepan and bring to a boil, stirring frequently. Cook, stirring constantly, until the mixture has thickened and reduced to about 2 cups. Remove from the heat and stir in 2 tablespoons Amaretto.

APPLE FILLING

YIELD: 2½ TO 3 CUPS

Peel, core, and thinly slice 5 apples. Place them in a large saucepan and add just enough water to cover. Bring to a boil and cook, stirring, occasionally, until the apples are very soft. Drain well and transfer to a medium bowl. Mash the apples with a wooden spoon or potato masher. Add ½ cup powdered sugar, 2 tablespoons Amaretto, 1 tablespoon fresh lemon juice, 1 tablespoon grated lemon zest, and ⅛ teaspoon ground nutmeg and stir until well blended.

CHOCOLATE CHEESECAKE FILLING

YIELD: 3 TO 3½ CUPS

In a large bowl, combine 1 pound room-temperature cream cheese, ¾ cup unsweetened cocoa powder, and ½ cup granulated sugar and beat until smooth and creamy. Beat in 4 large eggs one at a time, beating well after each addition. Beat in 2 tablespoons chocolate syrup.

COCONUT-PECAN FILLING

YIELD: 2½ TO 3 CUPS

Combine 1 cup evaporated milk, 3 large egg yolks, 1 cup granulated sugar, ½ cup vegetable shortening, and 1 teaspoon coconut flavoring in a large saucepan and cook over medium-low heat, stirring, until thick, 10 to 12 minutes. (Do not let the mixture boil.) Remove from the heat and stir in 1 cup flaked coconut and 1 cup chopped pecans. Let cool.

LEMON FILLING

YIELD: 2 TO 2½ CUPS

In a large bowl, combine 4 large eggs and 2 cups granulated sugar and beat until thick and light-colored. Beat in ⅓ cup all-purpose flour, 6 tablespoons lemon juice concentrate, and 1 teaspoon grated lemon zest. (This filling is to be poured over a partially baked crust and then baked until set and firm to the touch.)

PUMPKIN CHEESECAKE FILLING

YIELD: 3¼ TO 4 CUPS

In a large bowl, combine 11 ounces room-temperature cream cheese and ⅔ cups granulated sugar and beat until smooth and creamy. Beat in 16 ounces solid-pack pumpkin, 3 large eggs, 1½ teaspoons ground cinnamon, and 1 teaspoon vanilla extract (or another flavoring of your choice).

VANILLA SUGAR

YIELD: 1½ TO 2 CUPS

Rinse a vanilla bean in cold water and dry thoroughly with paper towels. Put 1½ to 2 cups sugar in a pint jar, add the vanilla bean, and shake well. Let stand for a few days, shaking the jar occasionally, before using the flavored sugar. Replenish the jar as you use it.

Here are almost twenty-one ideas for bar cookie crusts. (These are to be spread or patted into the bottom of a baking pan and partially baked before a topping or filling is spread over the crust and baked until done.) But, in fact, these should provide you with ideas for dozens of crusts. Any of these combinations can be varied according to your personal taste. For example, in a recipe that calls for all-purpose flour, you could substitute whole wheat flour, rice flour, or even buckwheat flour for some (usually no more than about a quarter) of the white flour. Or use vegetable shortening in place of butter in a crust. Or replace granulated sugar with brown sugar or raw sugar. Use your favorite nuts in any nut crust, or your favorite cookies in a crumb crust. And of course you can also change the flavoring, substituting another extract for vanilla, adding a liqueur, and so forth.

Use your imagination, but do keep one guideline in mind. If you are changing the crust in a favorite recipe, be sure to replace it with a similar crust, one that "matches" the filling or topping as in the original recipe. A filling that is very runny before it is baked, for example, needs the right kind of crust to support the unbaked filling. A crust that takes a long time to bake will not be cooked if combined with a topping that takes only minutes to bake. Keep baking times in mind when you are experimenting. Have fun!

See Bar Cookies in the text for basic procedures for combining particular ingredients to make a crust.

1
1 cup all-purpose flour
½ cup powdered sugar
6 tablespoons butter
1 tablespoon heavy cream

2
3 cups all-purpose flour
1 cup granulated sugar
1 cup butter
4 large eggs, separated
2 large egg yolks
½ teaspoon salt

3
16 graham crackers, crushed
½ cup granulated sugar
¼ cup butter

4
1 cup all-purpose flour
¾ cup granulated sugar
½ cup butter
⅓ cup milk
1 large egg
¾ teaspoon Amaretto

5
1 cup all-purpose flour
½ cup butter
¼ teaspoon salt

6
24 gingersnaps, crushed
¼ cup powdered sugar
½ cup canola oil

7
2 cups all-purpose flour
¼ cup granulated sugar

½ cup butter
¼ cup walnuts, ground fine

8

1½ cups whole wheat flour
¾ cup butter
2 tablespoons granulated sugar

9

1¼ cups all-purpose flour
½ cup vegetable shortening
¼ teaspoon salt
3 tablespoons ice water

10

1 cup all-purpose flour
½ cup powdered sugar
½ cup butter
½ cup shredded coconut
¼ teaspoon salt

11

1½ cups all-purpose flour
⅔ cup granulated sugar
½ cup butter
3 large egg yolks
2 tablespoons milk

12

1⅓ cups all-purpose flour
½ cup packed light brown sugar
⅓ cup butter
½ teaspoon baking powder
½ cup almonds, chopped

13

2 cups all-purpose flour
3 tablespoons powdered sugar
2 large egg yolks
1 teaspoon instant coffee
   crystals
1 tablespoon water

14

1⅓ cups crushed gingersnaps
¼ cup packed light brown sugar
2 tablespoons butter
3½ ounces macadamia nuts,
   ground fine
1½ teaspoons crystallized ginger, chopped

15

1 cup all-purpose flour
¼ cup light brown sugar
6 tablespoons butter
½ cup pecans, chopped fine
¼ teaspoon salt

16

1⅓ cup all-purpose flour
½ cup packed light brown sugar
⅓ cup butter
½ teaspoon baking powder
¼ cup hazelnuts, ground fine

17

1 cup all-purpose flour
½ cup packed light brown sugar
½ cup butter
¼ teaspoon ground cloves
½ teaspoon ground ginger
¼ teaspoon ground nutmeg

18

1½ cups all-purpose flour
½ cup butter
¼ teaspoon salt
2½ tablespoons warm water

19

2 cups all-purpose flour
¼ cup granulated sugar
½ cup butter
½ cup walnuts, ground fine

20

2 cups all-purpose flour
2 cups packed light brown sugar
1 cup butter

21

1 cup all-purpose flour
¾ cup packed light brown sugar
⅓ cup butter
2 large egg yolks
1 cup shredded coconut